COACHING THE 5-3-2

with a Sweeper

P. 53

By Eugenio Fascetti and Romedio Scaia

Library of Congress Cataloging - in - Publication Data

Fascetti, Eugenio and Scaia, Romedio
  Coaching the 5-3-2 with a Sweeper
Original title :Il Modulo Di Gioco 5:3:2".

ISBN No. 189094624-9
Library of Congress Cataloging Number 99070334
Copyright © July 1999

This book was originally published by Edizioni Nuova Prhomos.

Art Direction and Graphic Design
Kimberly N. Bender

Editing and Proofing
Bryan R. Beaver

REEDSWAIN INC.
612 Pughtown Road • Spring City, Pennsylvania 19475
1-800-331-5191 • www.reedswain.com

Table of Contents

Preface

I n this book Eugenio Fascetti traces the history of soccer patterns of play, particularly of the 5:3:2.

Of course he is aware of the fact that the perfect pattern of play, the one that can always guarantee a win, does not exist: each pattern has its own advantages and disadvantages and may be thwarted by adequate countermeasures. Any pattern can be successful if you have a team of champions: in fact it is the quality of the players that makes the difference.

Soccer is an ever changing sport, but it sometimes goes back to its origins and, like a musician, plays new or old music by updating it and adding endless variations. Thanks to his long and fruitful career as a coach, Fascetti teaches the need to be flexible, versatile, and to change schemes according to team, match, needs of the moment, and human resources. Never stick obstinately to an unchangeable vision of play. You cannot win by playing only in one way: the ability to change is fundamental, by studying the opponent and making the most of his weaknesses.

Every team must be familiar with more than one pattern of play and be ready to use them with chameleon-like ability, identifying the various parts each player must perform time after time. From "organized chaos" to chamaleonism: this is what better exemplifies Fascetti's soccer development.

Soccer is dynamism and continuous evolution: those who cling to a rigid vision of play and never change end up being inevitably overcome, as every team soon learns how to counter them.

I agree with another view of Fascetti's: at the beginning of the season, the coach must have a clear pattern of play in mind and choose the most suitable players according to it. If this is not possible, then he must choose the most suitable pattern according to the characteristics of the players he has.

In this book Fascetti goes over the various tactical patterns from their origins to modern times, showing how many of them repeat themselves or are closely related. He also shows how it is possible to change them with a few moves and adapt them to the needs of the match. Also very interesting are the illustrations of the patterns of play of the best national teams and clubs in history, where he points out the development and the contribution of the different soccer schools among which the Dutch of the 70s was probably the most important: after that soccer revolution nothing has ever been the same.

In the 5:3:2 coaching section he explains the tactics and teaches how to carry out the pattern through a detailed coaching program, with a long sequence of exercises and drills designed to develop in the players the necessary automatic movements.

This is an interesting and valuable book for coaches and for all those who wish to know more and get familiar with the 5:3:2 pattern of play.

Giorgio Tosatti

Foreword

This book intends to focus on studying, knowing and applying the 5:3:2 pattern of play. This entails a reference to the pattern it derived from, then to the origin of the latter and so forth back to the beginnings of soccer.

Analyzing the schemes and studying their evolution, we can see how each play pattern can be read as a transformation or development of the preceding one: this is why we could have the impression of finding modern patterns in "primitive" soccer. However, all those that we can consider play pattern recurrences are different thanks to their transformations and developments: each one restyles and introduces innovations to the original pattern.

This happens because patterns are not rigid schemes on paper: they come to life on the soccer field, according to factors such as individual players, the opponent, field conditions and so forth. Thanks to the dynamism of the conditions and factors to which they are applied, play patterns cannot be rigid and unambiguous: on the contrary, they continuously change and develop into new ones.

A pattern of play cannot work by itself, but it can be crucial depending on two fundamental factors:

* its flexibility to adjust to different teams, situations and players, even within the same match;

* the players applying it: their ability is instrumental in making it successful.

We believe that it is important for the players to be familiar with the 5:3:2 pattern of play as it is fundamental in today's soccer, but only as one of the possible tactical options which can be more or less effective depending on the skills of the individual players. In fact, this is the great and revolutionary teaching of modern soccer: no rigid schemes, but flexible ones according to the ever changing situations of teams, matches, results requirements and human resources.

The team must be familiar with many patterns of play and have the mental ability to choose them according to particular needs. Therefore, the coach has two tasks: a practical one, consisting of teaching the patterns of play and how to apply them, and a mental one, aimed at creating a "chameleon-like" kind of player who can carry out all the patterns of play.

This also happens in individual sports such as tennis: the real champion can also win by changing tactics, which he can do only if he knows different ways of playing. Just think of the players with a powerful serve:

those who limit themselves to taking advantage only of this resource, unable to make use of other tactics, have never gone very far. Boris Becker has never been able to perform very well on clay courts as he could not adjust his play on them. On the other hand, Venus Williams, a young tennis player, could beat an experienced Sanchez on the latter's favorite court not by using her awesome power, but by waiting for her opponent at the back of the court and playing topspins, taking advantage of the clay court slowness.

Other examples could be given from other sports and the conclusion would still be the same: a player does not win in only one way, but through his ability to adapt and change.

This implies knowledge of the available solutions, and so of the patterns: the ability to adapt and apply them, but not always in the same way. The mind of the players must be trained to make them flexible or, as said above, "chameleon-like".

In theory, a pattern of play could become invincible by itself only if the team were made up of stars but, as we have seen with tennis, not even a champion can win if he always makes use of the same tactics.

Modern soccer has shown that dynamism and evolution are the greatest revolution of the 80s: it would be a big mistake to ascribe almost magical powers to just one pattern of play or tactical solution.

The "pattern of play" is "the arrangement of the players on the field with the respective roles they have been given".

In order to be functional, any pattern of play must provide for a uniform occupation of the spaces, adapt to the various situations of play (for example, changing from the "5:3:2" to the "3:5:2" during the same match) and provide for a logical employment of the players in their respective roles.

The first decision to be made by the coach at the beginning of the season is what pattern of play he wants his team to apply.

There may be two options:

1. the coach already has in mind a pattern of play, according to which he chooses those players who better adapt to his tactics;

2. he decides to adopt a pattern of play to suit the players he currently has at his disposal.

It is always risky to think of adapting a pattern of play to players who are unsuitable for it, even if there is nothing to prevent the coach from doing so and, after adequate checks, thinking better of it.

After the "pure zone" boom and the adequate countermeasures taken to defeat such patterns of play, many coaches started to line up their team on the field in a more cautious way by adding an extra back, taking him from the midfield, and by placing behind the defense a central back playing as a sweeper. Such tactical arrangements guaranteed fewer risks in the defensive phase and provided for quick counterattacks towards the opposing goal.

It was, and is, called the "5:3:2": it becomes the "3:5:2" when the team carrying it out gets possession of the ball and moves forward with the two side backs.

It is commonly thought that playing with a sweeper entails a very conservative and outdated arrangement: this must be reconsidered. In fact, the efficiency of this defensive arrangement is demonstrated not only by today's play, but also by historical consideration: in the last thirty years, all the teams that have won either a world or European cup have played with a sweeper, thus proving the importance of such a role.

Of course, the quality of the individual player is a crucial factor. If you have outstanding players, any play pattern - the "5:3:2" or the flat back four - can be successful, with or without a sweeper.

Introduction

This book intends to give theoretical and practical information on the "5:3:2" pattern of play and on the ways it can be applied.

With "pattern" we mean "how the players of a team are arranged".

In order to be functional it must provide for a uniform occupation of the spaces and a logical employment of the players in their respective roles.

The "5:3:2" is a pattern of play that is not rigid and coexists in today's soccer together with other patterns.

In fact, during a match there may be a need for different solutions as the situation may change due to the opponent's pattern of play. Only a team of chameleon-like players, able to put into practice the various play patterns, can react accordingly.

The history of soccer shows that reality is made up of evolution and dynamism: new patterns have evolved because of deficiencies in those that preceded them. Therefore this book deals with the "5:3:2" starting from its origins: Chapter One contains the tactical development of soccer from the beginning to this modern pattern of play.

At first, teams would play without patterns: the players were arranged within a theoretical pyramid.

The need to better define the different parts of a team determined the invention of the "method" in South America, with the division into defense, midfield and attack.

The second great change took place with Chapman in England in 1928: it was the "system", with an arrangement that can be compared with today's 3:4:3, where the four central players were placed at the corners of a square. This tactical solution remained unchanged until the post-war period when, to defeat the forwards' excessive power, a "sweeper" was introduced by moving one of the four central players to the back of the defense. Uruguay was the first national team to apply this solution in 1950, when it won the World Cup. In Europe, this new role of the sweeper was adopted by Switzerland and in Italy by Viani's Salernitana and Foni's Inter Milan.

The system with a sweeper came to an end when the great Hungary (1950/1954) invented the role of the "deep-lying center forward".

Then, Pelé's Brazil introduced the modern "4:2:4" or "4:4:2", giving up the "static" sweeper.

In the 60s, Herrera's Inter Milan and Rocco's A.C. Milan re-employed the sweeper, man-marking and counterattacking.

In the 70s there was the Dutch revolution with the birth of pressure, mobility, higher speed and the total player. The Dutch cycle finished at the end of the decade with the end of its outstanding players but left behind some important characteristics of today's soccer: pressure, mobility and search for the ball, which all imply the need to adopt different solutions.

In the 80s there was the birth of the "5:3:2", a modified version of the schemes of the 60s, but with the introduction of the "mobile sweeper".

Chapter One describes all the schemes with references to teams, coaches and matches. Chapters Two and Three focus on the "5:3:2" pattern, analyzing its theoretical aspects: aims, conditions for its application, ideal players, advantages and disadvantages, countermeasures and adaptation to different schemes.

Finally, Chapters Four and Five give practical advice with exercises and drills designed to help the team learn this pattern, its variations and countermeasures.

Abbreviations and Symbols

G.	Goalkeeper
R.B./L.B.	Right back/Left back
R.S.P./L.S.P.	Right side player/Left side player
R.D./L.D.	Right side defender/Left side defender
P.C.H.	Play-making center halfback
R.H./L.H.	Right halfback/Left halfback
R.W./L.W.	Right wing/Left wing
C.F.	Center forward
D.C.F.	Deep-lying center forward
●	Ball
④	Player/s
❼	Opponent/s
③ ●ᴡᴡᴡ	Movement with the ball
⑤ --------▶	Movement without the ball
③ ●	Player with the ball
❷ ●	Opposing player with the ball

HISTORICAL OUTLINE

The beginnings

Soccer was born in England around the middle of the 19th century in the high society set as an alternative to rugby. As a consequence of such origin, the eleven players making up the team had a markedly attacking arrangement: one goalkeeper, one fixed defender (also called the second goalkeeper) and nine forwards: nine players who attacked without any prearranged scheme.

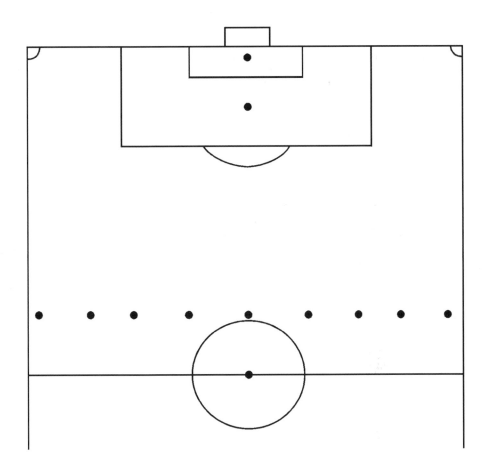

Diagram 1 - *original Arrangement*

All the changes that have taken place ever since and all the patterns and systems conceived and applied have shared the common aim of reinforcing the defense.

In 1870 the Scots were the first to feel the need of introducing two defenders: so their team was made up of a goalkeeper, a central defender, two side defenders and seven forwards. The task of these two new players, called backs, was to take the ball forward and link the two sections.

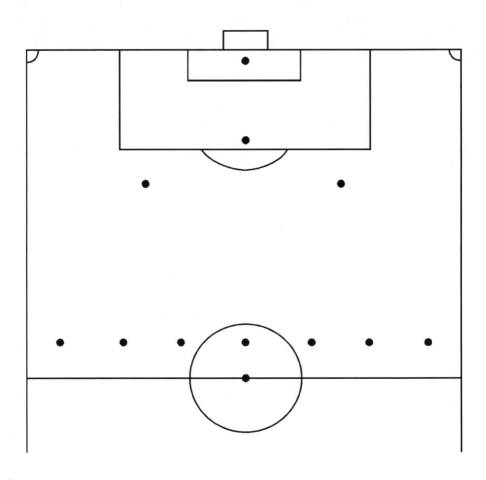

Diagram 2 - Arrangement of Scotland in 1870.

Five years later, it was Scotland again which conceived a more defensive arrangement by taking a player away from the attack and placing him next to the central defender: this was the so-called "upside down pyramid" scheme.

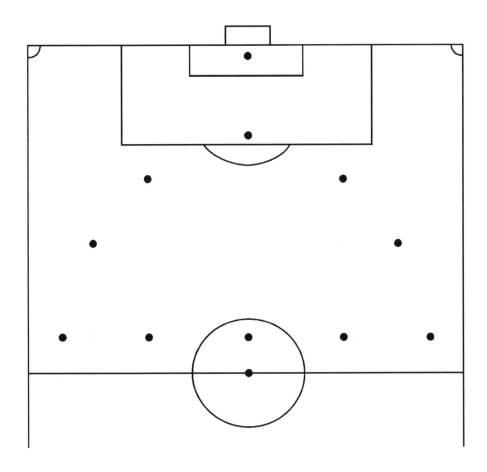

Diagram 3 - *Arrangement of Scotland in 1875: the "upside down pyramid".*

In modern terms, this scheme could also be defined as a "4:6": it established for the first time the principle that a defender should correspond to each forward.

However, at the beginning of the 1880s England regained possession of its honorary title of homeland of soccer by introducing the first real pattern of modern times: the "Method".

The method soon became an integral part of soccer, and when the latter was exported all over the world the method seemed to be one of the rules of the game.

In 1883 soccer stopped being a sport for rich people only. In England, Blackburn Olympic, a working class club, beat aristocratic Eton in the Cup final. This also meant the beginning of professional soccer: the new working class clubs needed their players to be free from work so they turned to patrons, joint-stock companies and lotteries for funding. Soccer became a mass sport and a vehicle for social integration.

The method

The method is characterized by a "5:5" arrangement, made up of the goalkeeper, two central backs, three halfbacks (one of them called the "play-making" center halfback), two side players, two wings and a forward. The two central backs must mark the opposing attackers and the two halfbacks the opposing wings, while the "play-making" center halfback acts as a link between the defense and the attack, playing the role of the "playmaker".

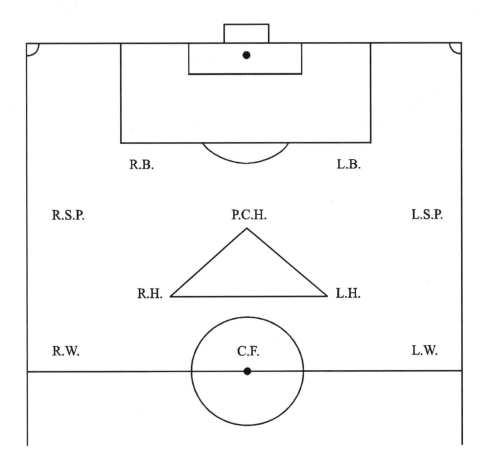

Diagram 4 - The "Method" arrangement.

This scheme is similar to the 5 player defense of the 5:3:2: if the P.C.H. becomes a sweeper and the two backs turn into marking players, then we have a 3 player defense which can play either along the same line (see Udinese F.C.) or with a sweeper. The method also contains other important characteristics of modern soccer:

1. zone play:

   each of the two backs controls an area and takes care of the attacker in the zone where he belongs: this is what the central defenders do in today's 4:4:2;

2. the side halfbacks take care of the opposing wings, thus anticipating the role of today's side backs, ready to defend but also to attack;

3. the method applies the off-side trap: according to a rule introduced in 1886 between the goalkeeper and the opposing attacker there had to be two defenders. So, it was enough for the method to make either back sprint forward in order to leave the opposing attacker off-side. The method was so effective that the International Board decided to change the rules, limiting to one the number of players between the goalkeeper and the opposing attacker for the latter not to be off-side. This rule remained unchanged until 1990.

The method influenced world soccer for over 50 years, developing and adapting itself according to the different soccer schools.

In Italy it was applied best by Pro Vercelli, a small town team, which reigned supreme from 1908 to 1922 also thanks to its conditioning training, influenced by its gymnastic club tradition.

In the years between the late 20s and the early 30s soccer underwent two extraordinary changes: one from the managerial point of view, the other from the tactical one.

The managerial change was brought about by Austrian soccer, which dominated the international scene from 1931 to 1933: it affirmed the importance of coaches and their techniques and, especially, the fundamental role of the coach.

The tactical change originated in England: it was called "the System" and was conceived by Chapman, coach for Arsenal F.C. from 1928.

"Double M" method

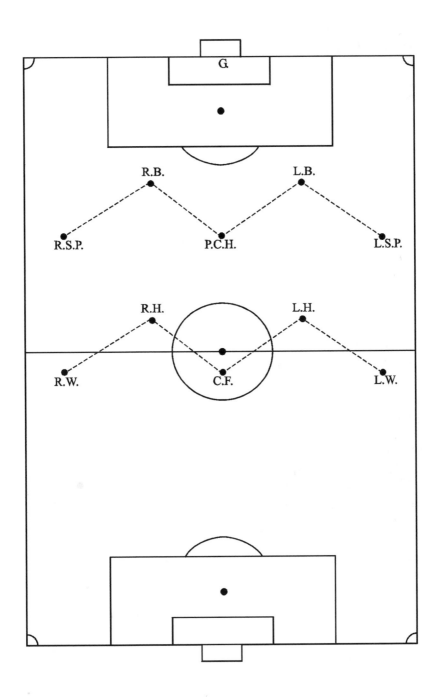

Diagram 5 - *Double M.*

In the method the most important role was played by the so called "Play-making center halfback".

He had to:

1. mark the opposing number 9;
2. start and make the play together with the "balancing" midfielder.

The two side players marked the two wings, while the backs actually acted as sweepers; the halfbacks marked their corresponding opponents. With a couple of moves such a scheme can easily be turned into a "5:3:2" or a "3:4:3".

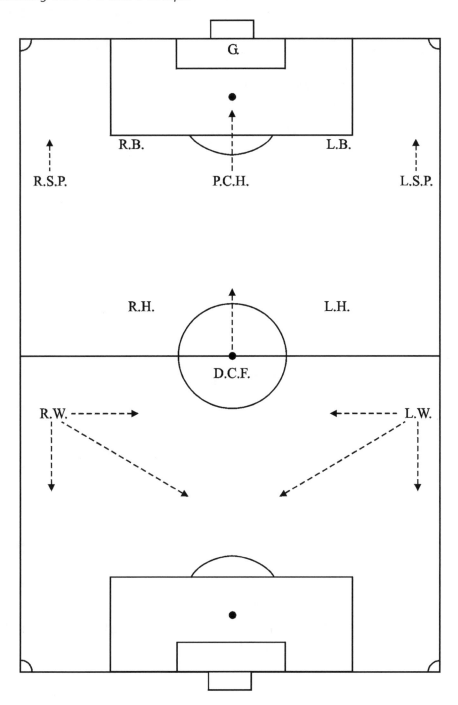

Diagram 6 - *Conversion into 5:3:2.*

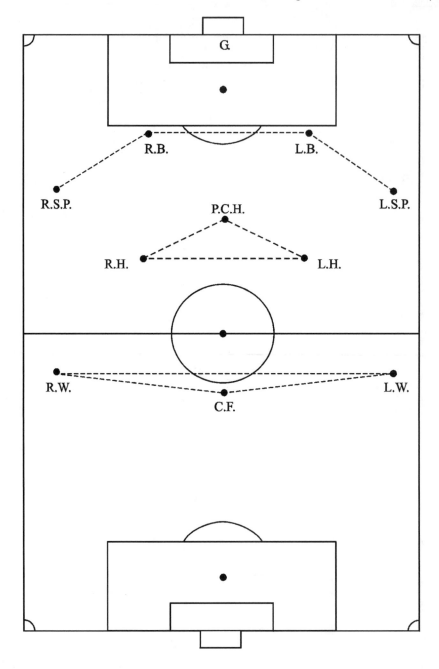

Diagram 7 - "4:3:3". The two backs turn into central backs. 3 player midfield forming a triangle with the top in the defensive position.

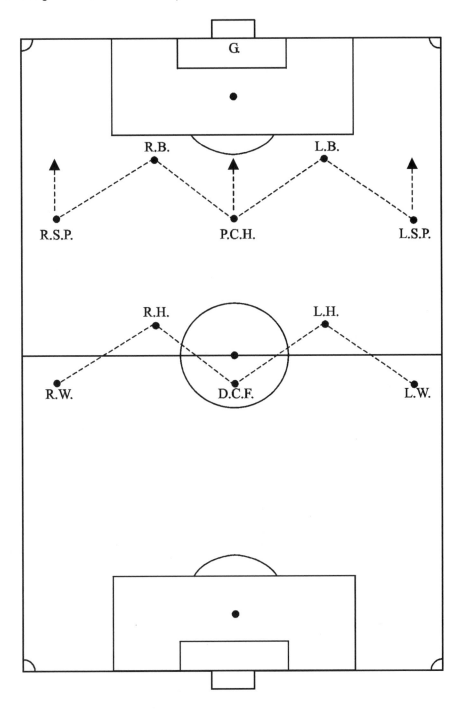

Diagram 8 - "5:2:3".

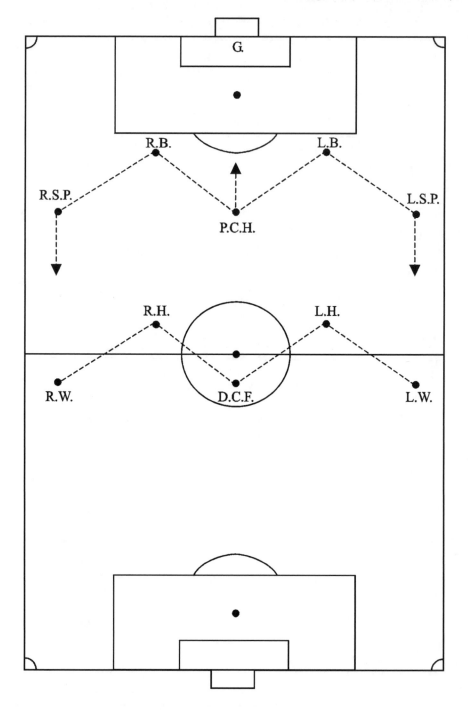

Diagram 9 - "3:4:3".

The "system" came to an end when Hungary beat traditionalist England with the two center forwards, who were actually midfielders: the real center forward, Hideguty, stepped back followed by the opposing stopper, thus enabling the two halfbacks to act as inside forwards and penetrate into the center of the attack:

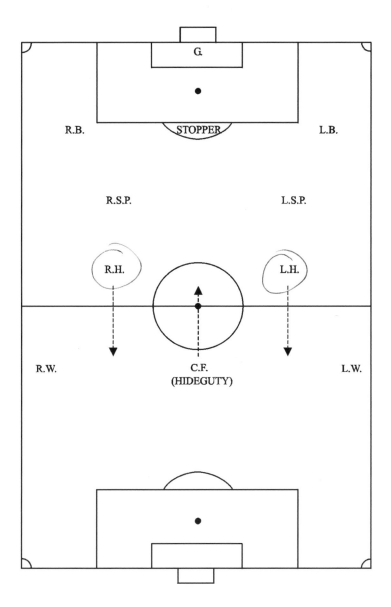

Diagram 10 - Hungary.

Brazil developed the "4:2:4", which later changed into the "4:4:2", then into the "4:3:3" (Pelé's great Santos):

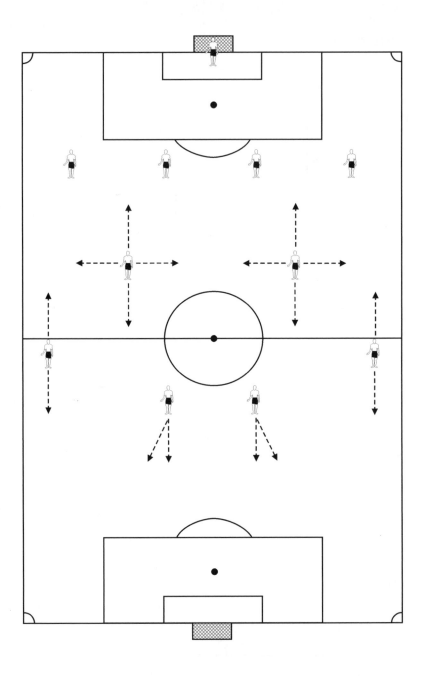

Diagram 11 - *The "4:2:4": 4 defenders arranged along the same line; 2 midfielders; 2 linkmen; 2 forwards.*

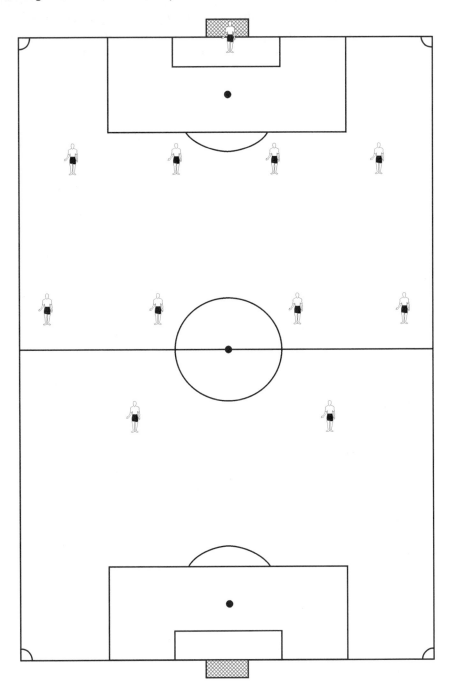

Diagram 12 - *The "4:4:2": 4 defenders; 4 midfielders; 2 forwards.*

Thanks to some tactical adjustment (the two central defenders are not along the same line: one man-marks an opponent, the other takes care of territorial marking), Brazil won the World Cup in Sweden in 1958.

The integral pure system

The following diagram shows the famous "box":

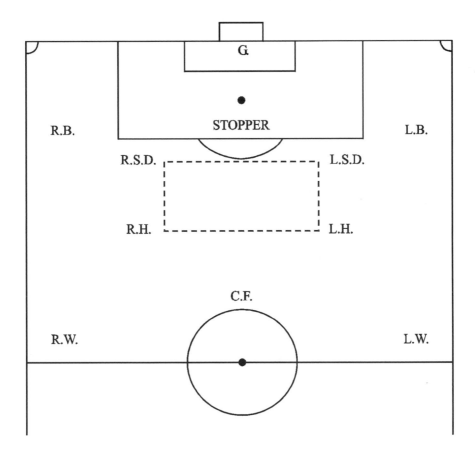

Diagram 13 - *The box.*

The "grande Torino"

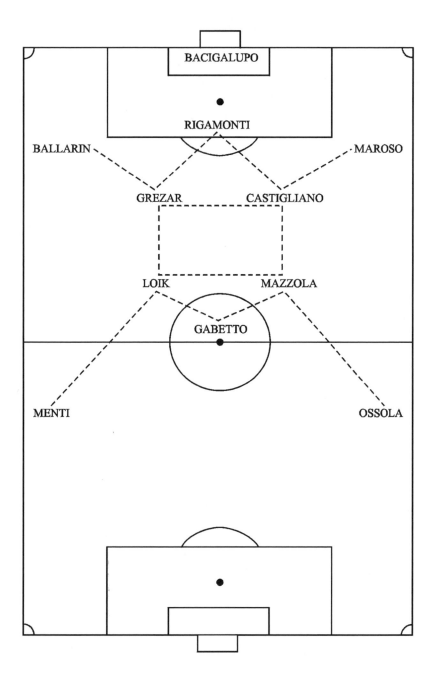

Diagram 14 - *The "grande Torino": W - M.*

The space-attacking 3:2:2:3 arrangement was first used by Torino, then nicknamed "grande" (great): all the midfielders were supposed to attack and shoot at goal.

We can easily imagine a kind of "5:3:2" (or "3:5:2") starting from the "W-M-shaped" tactical arrangement of this team, even if the side players man-marked the opposing wings and therefore could not pursue the attack as in the typical 5:3:2 and the attackers were made up of two pure wings and a center forward, if the latter stepped back to the midfield line.

This is the arrangement according to the "5:3:2":

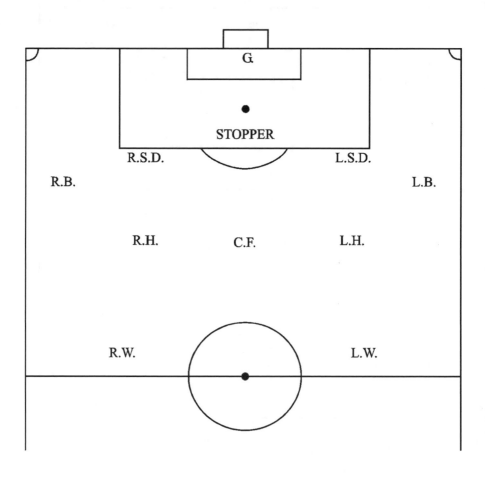

Diagram 15 - The "grande Torino": conversion into "5:3:2".

The two backs played on the sides, man-marking the opposing wings, while in the center the stopper marked the center forward. The two half-backs and the two inside defenders made up the midfield "box", with both an intercepting and play-making task, while the attacking wings took the action towards the goal-line, then crossed to the center forward.

Maroso was the first back in the world to participate in the attack.

They never passed the ball to their team-mates' feet, they made passes towards the spaces that were exploited through "cut-ins" and "diagonal" movements.

In the postwar period a less "integral" system was conceived. The defense was strengthened in order to counter the attack's excessive power. Switzerland applied defensive tactics by introducing the role of the sweeper and Uruguay did the same thing at the 1950 World Cup.

The system

The system was partly originated by the changes brought about by the off-side rule. Chapman decided to reinforce the defense and so he introduced the idea of man-marking with three defenders and a crowded midfield.

In particular:

- he pulled back the center halfback and placed him along the same line as the backs, thus turning him into a stopper; he placed the two backs more to the sides, so that the three opposing attackers were faced by three defenders;
- he placed the other two halfbacks more to the center, as a support to the defense: thus he created the famous "box", according to what was also called the "W-M shaped" arrangement.

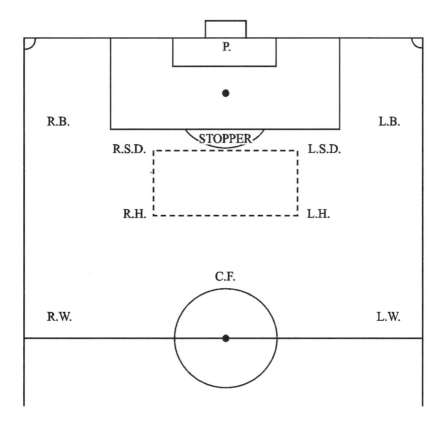

***Diagram 16** - The "System" arrangement.*

The great change was the strengthening of the defense. The backs did not defend the spaces any more, they marked the opponent with the ball: man-marking play was born.

The system arranged the players according to a 3:2:2:3 pattern, which can be easily compared to today's 3:4:3 even if in the latter the four central players can also be placed in differently shaped arrangements: diamond, upright or upside-down triangle, along the same line.

In Italy teams kept on playing according to the (partly updated) method throughout the 30s.

Edoardo Agnelli decided to import the system by hiring Chapman's assistant but the experiment failed and his successor, Caracano, maintained the method, introducing a change in the defense: he placed the backs more to the sides and pulled back along their line the center halfback, who kept the task of re-starting the action. This was a sort of system in embryo.

This tactic enabled the Italian national team coached by Pozzo to win the 1934 World Cup, the 1936 Berlin Olympics and the 1938 World Cup.

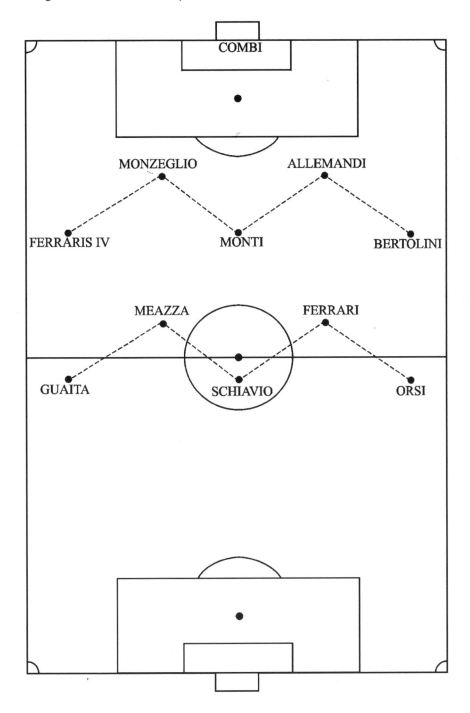

Diagram 17 - *The arrangement of Pozzo's Italy.*

Of course, Italy's achievements in the 30s were possible thanks to the exceptional quality of the players too: no system can be successful without the right players.

In Italy the system was applied in the 40s, first by Garbutt's Genoa and then by "grande" Torino which won four Italian league championships in a row, from 1945 to 1948.

"Grande" Torino was based on an aggressive and man-marking defense, with outstanding players like Valentino Mazzola, Loik, Gabetto, Rigamonti and Maroso.

The system in the postwar period

The system's weak point was the defense: its "one on one" arrangement could not resist mass attacks.

In Italy, tactical countermeasures were mostly conceived in small town clubs: Modena, Triestina and, especially Salernitana. Salernitana's Gipo Viani, perhaps one of modern soccer's most talented coaches, pulled back the halfback to man-mark the opposing center forward, thus enabling the stopper to play as a sweeper.

This was the beginning of what was to characterize Italian soccer: the so-called "catenaccio" (defensive tactics, literally "bolt", from the idea of blocking the opposing attack), exemplified best by Foni's Inter Milan in 1952 and 1953.

In that team the right wing (Armano, 7) marked the opposing left wing, thus enabling the right back (Blason, 2) to move to the back of the stopper (Giovannini, 5).

The arrangement by Foni can be compared to today's 4:4:2, even if it provides for a sweeper and a different arrangement in the midfield.

Diagram 18 - *The arrangement of Foni's Inter Milan.*

At the end of the 50s, Viani (A.C. Milan's coach) conceived something very similar to the 4:3:3: he made his midfielders play as backs and placed the sweeper in front of the stopper.

The "system" can be easily converted into today's "3:4:3" by changing the arrangement of the midfielders:

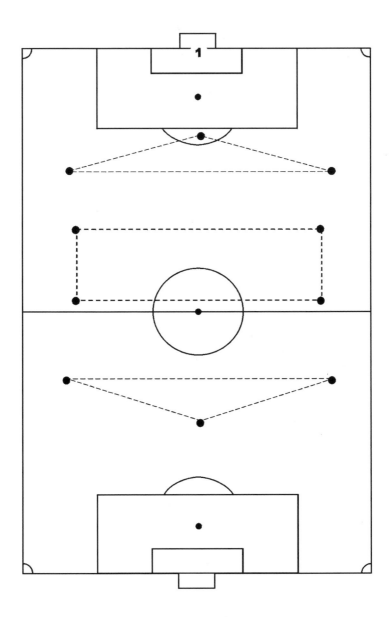

Diagram 19 - *The system.*

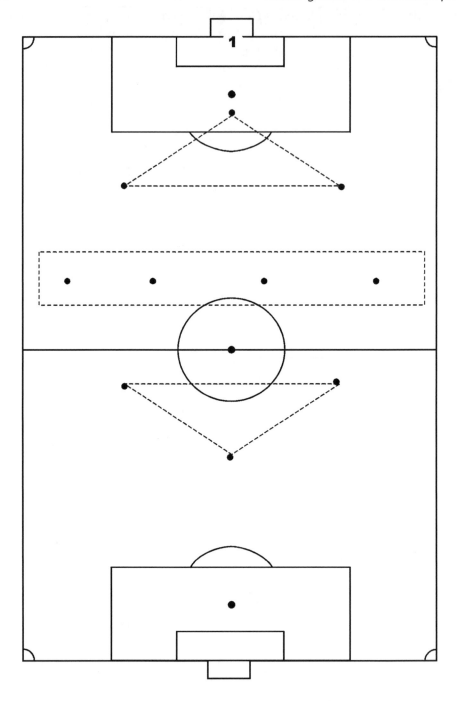

Diagram 20 - Conversion of the system into the "3:4:3".

The end of the system and the beginning of the 4:4:2 or 4:2:4

The system officially finished when Hungary beat England in 1953 and 1954: 6-3 in London and 7-1 in Budapest.

Hungary introduced two center forwards in this way:

- its real center forward stepped back, acting as a decoy for the opposing stopper;
- the two halfbacks acted as forwards and so did the wings, in the attacking phase.

This was the prototype of the 4:4:2 in the defensive phase and of the 4:2:4 in the attacking one.

The real 4:4:2 or 4:2:4 originated in Brazil in 1958, thanks to Pelé's Santos:

- four defenders arranged along the same line for "masked" zone-marking play.

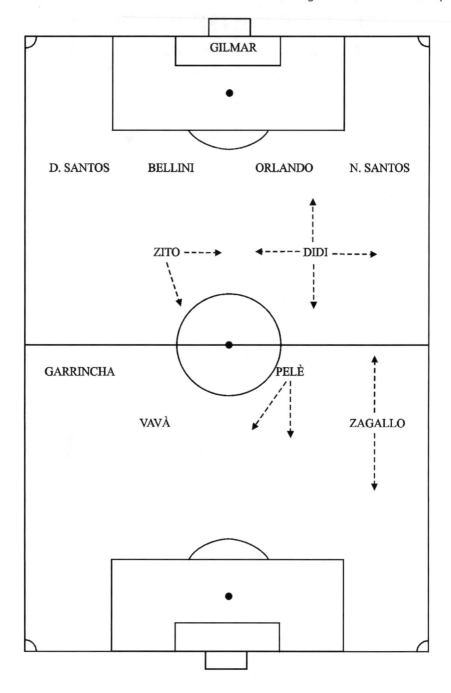

Diagram 21 *- The arrangement of Pelé's Brazil.*

   South American teams have played in the 4:4:2 or 4:2:4 pattern ever since, doing away with Uruguay's tactics which won the 1950 World Cup with the sweeper, Varela.

   Brazil won the 1958 and 1962 World Cups thanks to a "masked" sweeper and a zone-play arrangement, taken up by England in 1966 with the four midfielders placed in the shape of a diamond.

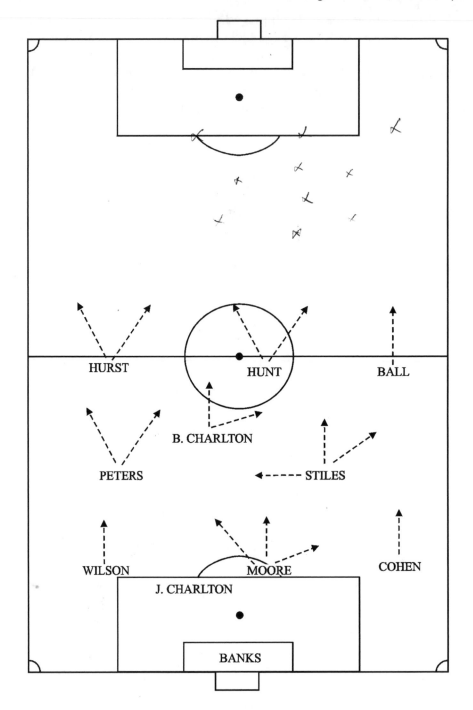

Diagram 22 - *The arrangement of 1966 England.*

Diagram 23 - *Scala's Parma, cup winner in 1992 and 1993.*

This new zone tactic was never typical of Italy. Apart from 1962 Amaral's Juventus, Vinicio's Naples, Marchioro's A.C. Milan and Liedholm's Rome, the 60s and the 70s were dominated by "catenaccio", with both backs and midfielders man-marking the opponents, plus a sweeper.

The outstanding coaches of these defensive tactics were Rocco (Padova, then A.C. Milan), Herrera (Inter Milan) and Trapattoni (Juventus).

At the end of the 60s there was a major change: the Dutch revolution and the development of total soccer, with the introduction of "pressure", "pressure zone" and "methodical off-side".

The Dutch revolution

At the end of the 60s Holland shook modern soccer with Rinus Michels and Kovacs.

While previously soccer had been based on marking the opponents, the new Dutch soccer focused on marking the space. The notion of "corridor" was introduced: the ball had to be passed towards the empty and long space which was necessarily present given the dimension of the soccer field. So, after focusing on the opponent and the ball, soccer started to consider the importance of the team-mates and space. This led to territorial marking: the opponent is marked in the area where one belongs. If a defender is obliged to change zones, a team-mate shifts to the abandoned zone.

Holland reigned supreme from 1969 to 1974: its best total player, Cruyff, was a real soccer playmaker. Yet, at the end, Holland lost to Germany in the World Cup final: once again, adequate countermeasures had been found.

The case of Holland confirms that genial, innovative and winning tactics do exist, but they need the right players and are not absolute: each tactic has a weak point, so countermeasures or other tactical answers will always be found. Never fossilize!

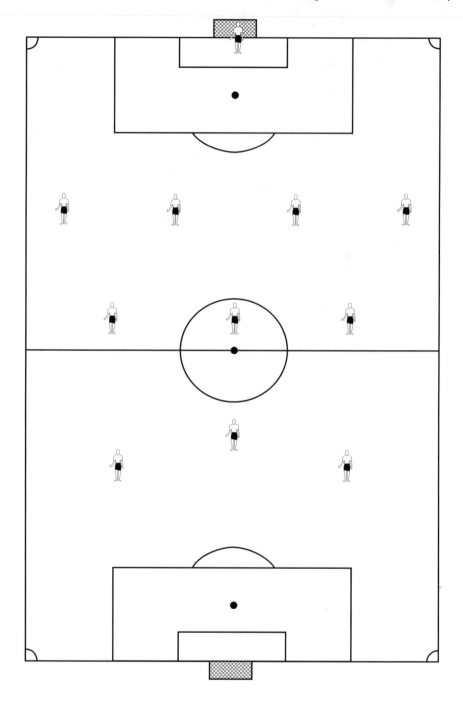

Diagram 24 - Holland's arrangement.

Holland played a decisive role in the development of modern soccer by introducing many changes:

1. The importance of group movement: for example, Holland's goalkeeper was the first to go out of his penalty area.

2. The exploitation of defenders in the attacking phase.

3. Versatility or total soccer.

4. Short play.

5. The importance of conditioning training.

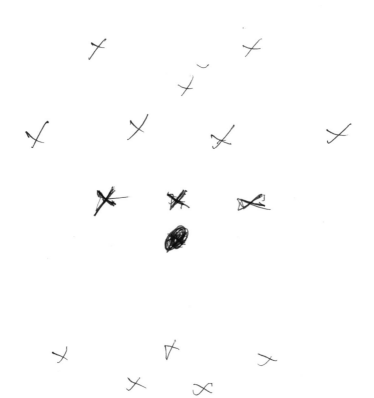

Real Madrid (3:4:3)

Diagram 25 - *Real Madrid's "3:4:3" pattern.*

Real Madrid's "3:4:3" can be easily converted into the "5:3:2":

Diagram 26 - *Real Madrid's pattern converted into the "5:3:2": Santamaria as a sweeper at the back of the defense, Santisteban and Di Stefano pulled back and positioned, respectively, along the defense and the midfield line.*

Soccer in the 80s

In the early 80s most teams applied zone play according to a 4:4:2 or 4:2:4 pattern, though each with some slight variations (see South American and English teams).

Holland adjusted its total soccer and balanced it with players from its former colonies, physically strong and tactically disciplined.

Italy, despite Vinicio's Naples and Liedholm's Rome achieving good results, still preferred Trapattoni's soccer: a typical "catenaccio" arrangement, but with some 4:3:3 oriented innovations (for instance, Causio was moved forward, near outstanding attackers like Boninsegna and Bettega). Italy's traditional allegiance to "catenaccio" existed until the end of the 80s, when Sacchi successfully applied the 4:4:2 in A.C. Milan.

Sacchi's great innovation consisted in the method of work, the extreme search for automatic movements and an increase in coaching activity. The limitation of Sacchi and his follower Zeman lies in their rigidity and difficulty in understanding soccer history's great lesson: soccer develops and adapts to the players, the situations and the opponents. Only zone play Coach Erickson seems to have this necessary flexibility.

Belgium 1980

At the 1980 European Cup Belgium introduced the following pattern of play in order to better defend itself from teams of a higher technical level: such tactics were truly successful.

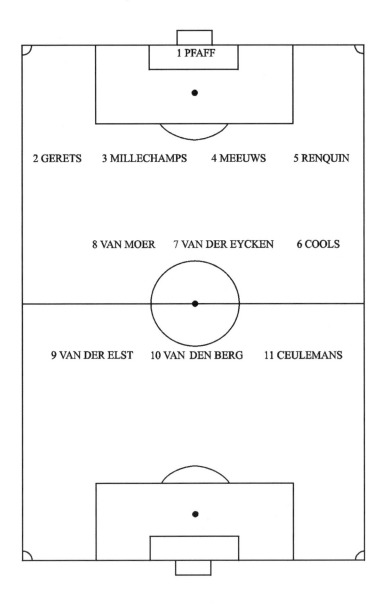

Diagram 27 - *The "4:3:3" pattern.*

Such a "4:3:3" pattern could be turned into a "5:3:2" when the team was attacked in the center. Player 5 goes and marks an opposing forward, player 4 acts as a sweeper and player 6 covers the left side:

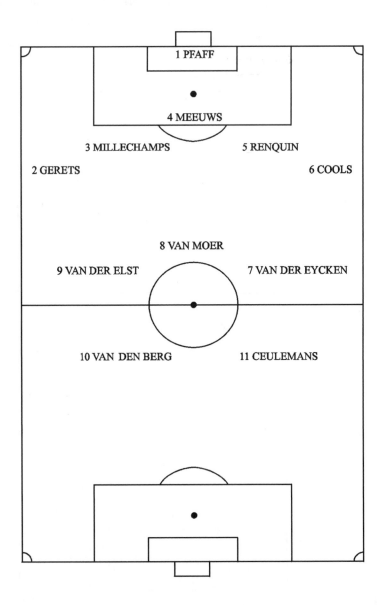

Diagram 28 - The "4:3:3" converted into the "5:3:2". Meeuws acted as a "sweeper" at the back of the defense, Cools stepped back to the defensive line, Van Der Elst stepped back on the right side, Van Moer moved to the center of the midfield line.

As opposed to what happened in the "method", in the "system" the two backs mark the opposing wings and the stopper marks the center forward. The four players making up the "box" make the play and the two wings and the center forward play in the attack.

Little by little one of the two wings, mostly the right one, reverses his field of action after the introduction of the sweeper.

While the goalkeepers were used to playing only on the goal line before, with the "system" they had to improve their challenges.

— Simmons
— manson
= Richy
— Cotter
— Gillard
— keefer
— millar
— clarke
— Farran
— Krongle \
— Bjurman
— Gruneau
— Hornita
— Drwin
— Chambers
— Symons
— Forward
— Suger

Krongle (Bjurman)   manson (Symons)

Gruneau (Forward)   Simmons (Darwin/Farran)   Ricky (millar)

Farran (Richey)   Clarke (Darwin)

Gillard (millar)   Cotter (Clarke)   keefer (millar)

Suger

Strikers   Mids)   Omids
Manson   Simmons   Ricky
Krongle   Farran   Fernand
Bjurman   Richey   Hornita
Symons   Drwin   Gruneau
Ricky   Clarke
Forward   Chambers
Chambers

Trapattoni's Juventus (1985)

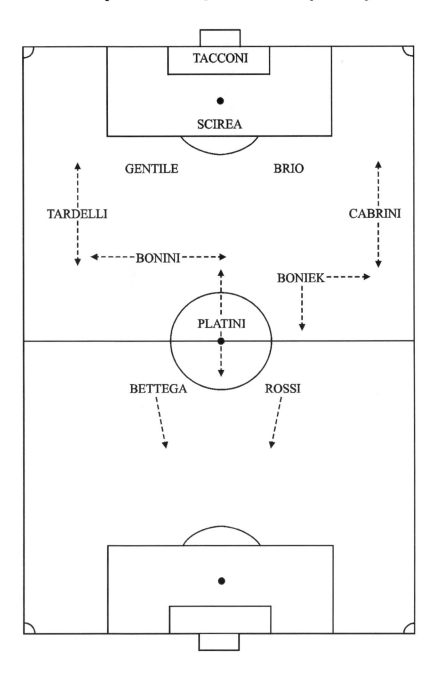

Diagram 29 - *Juventus in 1985 (5:3:2).*

This arrangement could be turned into a "3:4:3":

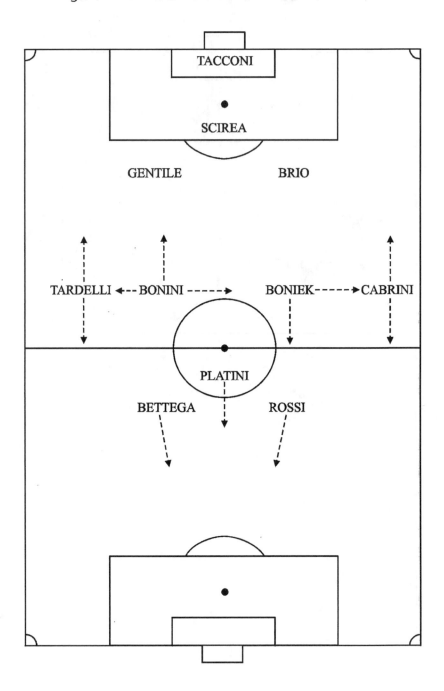

Diagram 30 - *Juventus converted into a "3:4:3".*

The 90s and the 5:3:2

The 4:4:2, though widely used, does have a weak point: the central pair of the four defenders.

Once again, the need for solutions has generated an innovation: the 5:3:2, conceived by Belgium.

With these tactics the role of the sweeper can be recovered as a support to the two central defenders when two opposing forwards attack (see diagram 28: Belgium's "5:3:2" pattern).

The 5:3:2 was immediately adopted by Brazil in the 1990 World Cup, by Germany and, in Italy, by Scala who was the first to apply it in his Parma team (see diagrams 21, 36 and 23: arrangements of Brazil, Germany and Scala's Parma).

In the next pages we are going to analyze the "5:3:2" in detail: the third chapter is about its teaching aspects, while the fourth contains exercises and schemes for implementing the 5:3:2.

However, before proceeding to that specific part, we would like to briefly summarize what we have meant to demonstrate so far:

1. the constant evolution of soccer and its continuous changes of tactics because of the players and their increasing athletic power;
2. the continuous redefinition of patterns, in embryo since the beginnings of soccer;
3. the need to know more solutions in order to choose the best according to:
   - the players of the moment
   - the opponents
   - specific ranking requirements;
4. last, but not the least, the absence of the absolute and perfect scheme or pattern.

Italy 1990

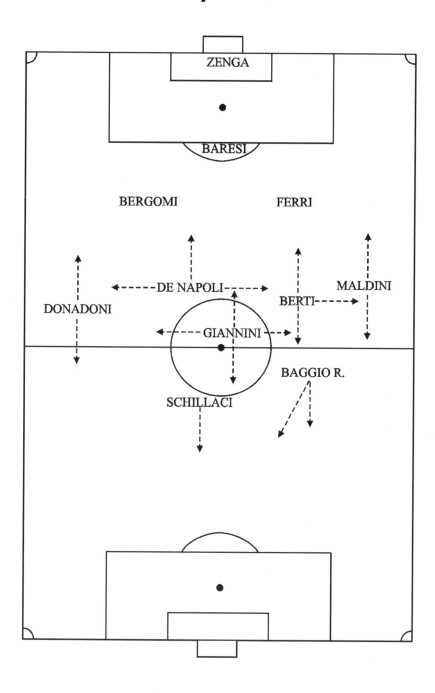

Diagram 31 - *Italy's national team at the 1990 World Cup.*

Inter Milan (5:3:2)

At present, in Italy the teams that exemplify best the 5:3:2 are Inter Milan and Atalanta: they show a careful defense and quick counterattacks. Thanks to these tactics, Atalanta's away wins are numerous while it encounters more difficulties in home matches when it plays against well covered defenses.

On the contrary, Inter Milan wins both away and at home because, differently from Atalanta, it has truly outstanding players.

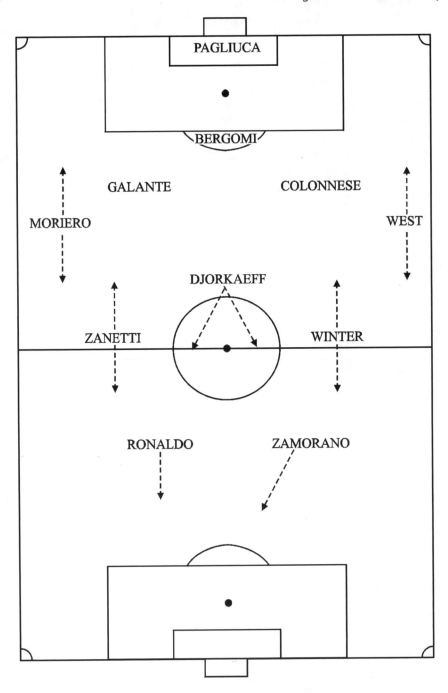

Diagram 32 - *Inter Milan's "5:3:2" (1997/1998 season).*

Fiorentina (3:4:3)

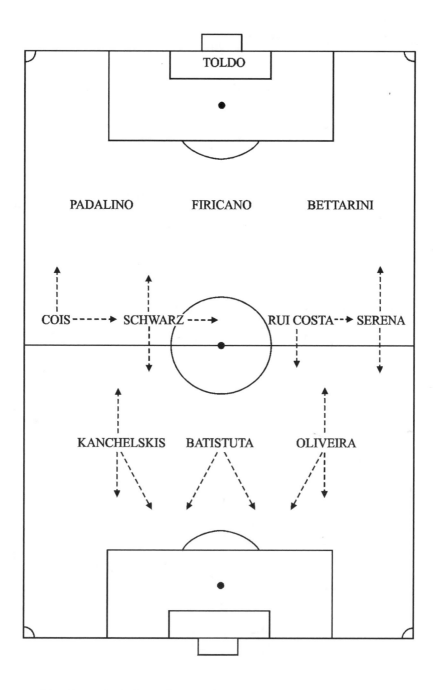

Diagram 33 *- Fiorentina's "3:4:3" (1997/1998 season).*

This can be easily converted into a "5:3:2":

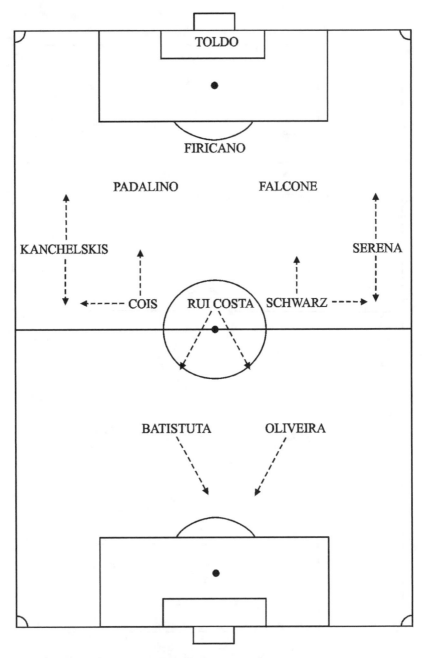

Diagram 34 - Fiorentina's arrangement converted into the "5:3:2".

It can also be converted into a "4:4:2":

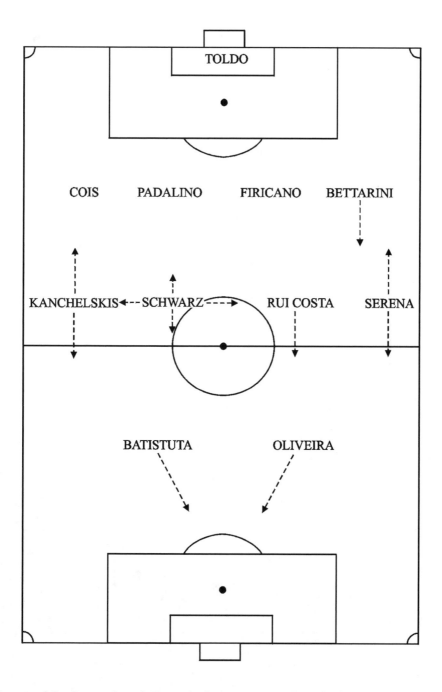

Diagram 35 - *Conversion of Fiorentina's arrangement into the "4:4:2".*

The "4:3:3" becomes the "3:5:2" by pulling back a wing who very often had to take care of defensive tasks and by advancing a back that is no longer needed to mark the opposing wing.

The German national team chose this starting arrangement at the 1990 World Cup in Italy:

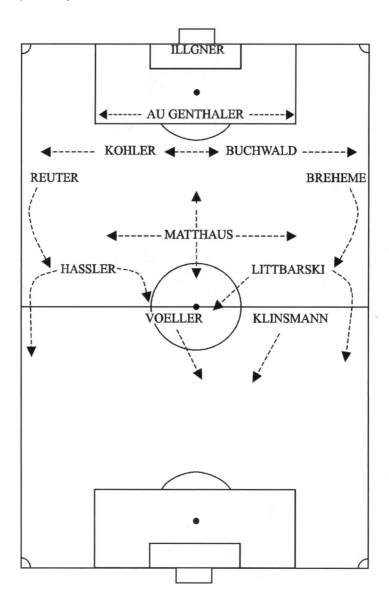

Diagram 36 - The German national team at the 1990 World Cup.

CHAPTER II

TACTICS

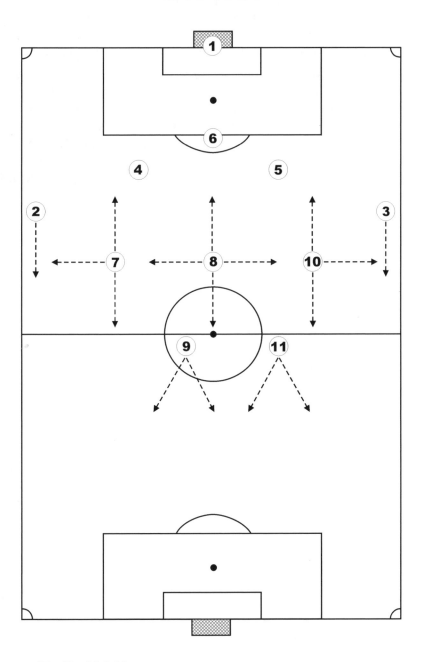

Diagram 37 - The "5:3:2".

In zone defense the three central defenders apply territorial marking of their opponents.

In man-marking defense two defenders man-mark the opposing attackers while the third one plays as a sweeper at the back.

The two side players must have great athletic strength in order to support the midfielders from the sides, reach the goal line and cross to the forwards, then return to the defensive position (even though most of the time they are helped by a midfielder who stays behind to cover them).

The role of the three midfielders is played by the two halfbacks (whose task is to intercept the opponents and build the attack) and by a so-called central playmaker who can play "forward" or "backward" according to the match situation. This is usually the midfielder with the greatest skills.

The "5:3:2" arrangement is completed by two central forwards who must give the ball to each other through mostly short passes and penetrate the opposing defense centrally.

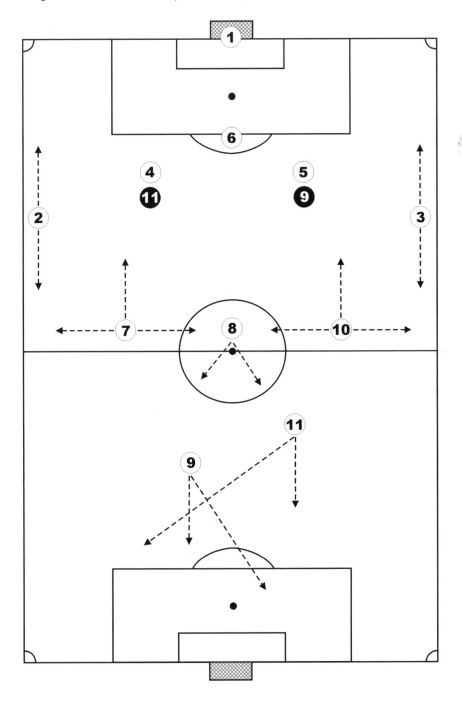

Diagram 38 - The "5:3:2" with man-marking defense and a sweeper at its back.

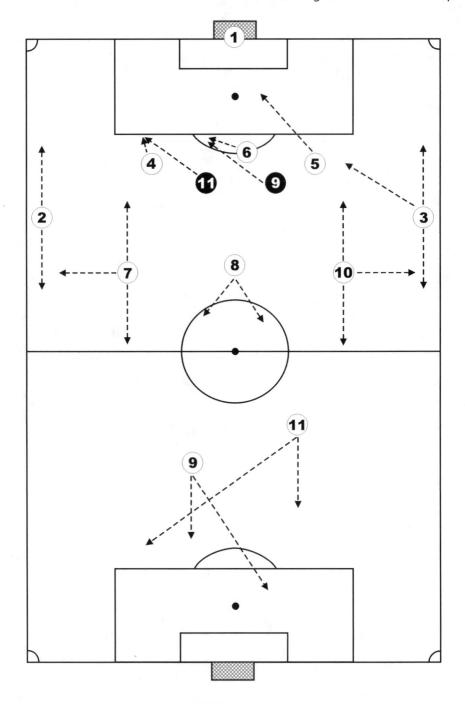

Diagram 39 - The "5:3:2" with zone-marking defense (player 5 can shift to the "sweeper" position).

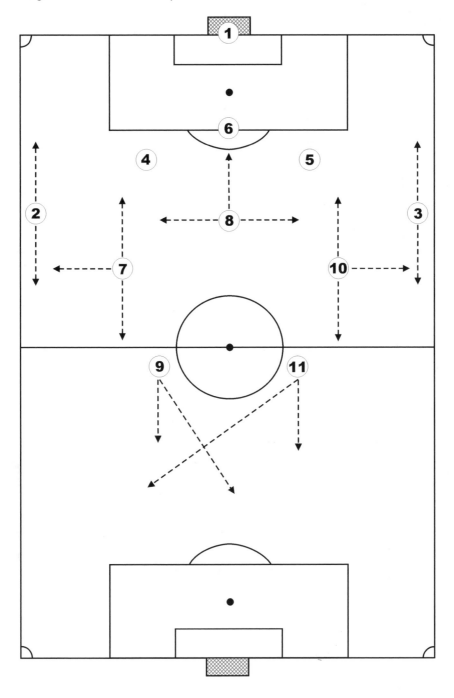

Diagram 40 - The "5:3:2" with the playmaker in front of the defense.

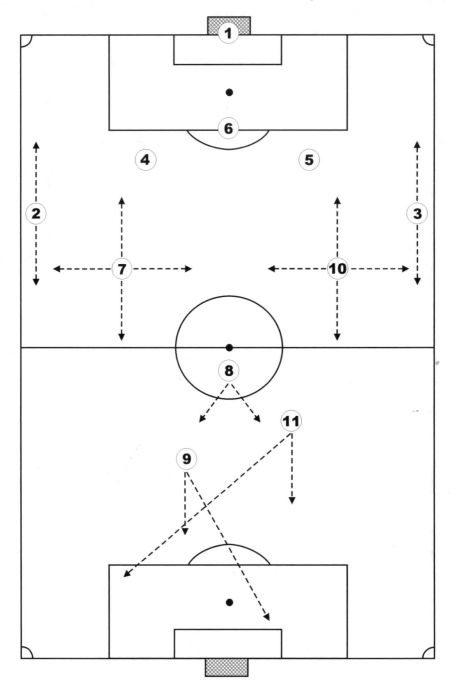

Diagram 41 - The "5:3:2" with the playmaker playing more forward with respect to the position of the halfbacks.

CHAPTER III

TEACHING THE 5:3:2

Characteristics of the players in the 5:3:2

❏ **Central defenders**
They man-mark the forwards or they control the center-right and the center-left areas in the zone-marking arrangement. They must be able to tackle and anticipate the opponent; it is better if one of them is good in the air and the other is quick and nimble in his movements.

❏ **The sweeper**
As he is the last defender, he must possess a good positional sense and be able to cover up for his team-mates' possible mistakes. When the team has possession of the ball he should take part in the attack, then recover behind his team-mates when the opponents start their attack.

❏ **Side players**
They must carry out a lot of work, defending and moving forward on attack. They are usually characterized by very good athletic qualities, ability to recover and remarkable speed. It is not so easy to cover such a big part of the field and have the necessary clearness of mind to make good cross-passes or shots at goal.

❏ **The playmaker**
He is responsible for maintaining the team's balance. He must possess good skills and be a good interceptor. If he has very good skills and scoring ability, then he can play in front of the two halfbacks, supporting the forwards; if his outstanding qualities are determination and tactical sense then he can play in front of the defense, allowing the penetration of the halfbacks.

❏ Halfbacks or inside forwards

They are usually dynamic players able to defend or attack; it is better if they can also cover in the midfield.

They are very important in double-teaming on the sides and in deep penetration.

They usually apply zone-marking.

❏ Forwards

The ideal pair of forwards must have different characteristics: one of them should be tall, strong and dynamic, able to protect the ball and win possession in the opposing penalty area; the other should be more dynamic: agile, creative, a good passer and ready to penetrate starting from the midfield.

Disadvantages of the
4 defenders along the same line

1. If the opposing team quickly shifts from the defensive to the attacking phase, then the defenders who have moved forward onto the attack do not have the time to return and quickly form the four-player defensive line again.

2. Once the four-player defense line has been passed, the goalkeeper is unprotected.

3. The four-player defensive line can be passed by:
   a. penetration on the wings and crosses behind the defensive line;
   b. deep pass, control of the ball and a further pass to a third player sprinting behind the defensive line;
   c. switching the play front with diagonal passes towards the opposite side of the field to bypass the defense line.

The team should be able to play choosing from different solutions in order to give the opponents very few reference points. Unpredictability, that is a "chameleon-like" team, is one of the most important cards that can be played during a match.

The team's ability and flexibility to change during the match entails the ability of the individual players to adapt to any possible tactical solution. Therefore it is important to:

A. immediately analyze and understand certain situations (the opponents' pattern, their shape, their strengths, etc...);

B. solve the problem in the shortest possible time (many players encounter difficulties because they are not used to reasoning);

C. play the match with maximum awareness, that is:
   a. be able to see one's own position with respect to:
      1. the ball;
      2. one's own teammates;
      3. the opponents;
      4. the technical-tactical skills of one's own teammates and of the opponents;
      5. the reference points of the field;
   b. be able to always choose from the most important reference points;
   c. make decisions and carry out adequate movements.

There can be no team play without patterns and tactical awareness. With "patterns" we mean the way a team is arranged on the field. From the "pyramid" to today's "3:4:3" there has always been a rotation of patterns, according to whether the aim was defense or attack. There are no absolute winning patterns: very good patterns do exist, sometimes also in contrast to one another, which all teams and any individual player should be able to apply.

In the pyramid pattern, the team was arranged carelessly and without any logical sense, just applying an empirical pattern. Instead, with the "METHOD" the team was arranged by following a certain logic: the defense was taken care of first, then the midfield and finally the attack. In this way, the three so-called "sections" of the team were formed.

From the "method" to the "system" the distance was short: from the first "integral" system (five defenders, two midfielders and three forwards) a new tactical development moved a player to the back of the defense, with the role of sweeper which, in our opinion, is a key role.

Inter Milan's coach, Foni, imported the role of the "sweeper" and won two Italian League Championships in a row.

The necessity of having a sweeper came from the need to stop the excessive power of the attacks.

Advantages and disadvantages of the "5:3:2"

Play organization is based on two essential requirements: knowledge of the available players and of the pattern we want the team to adopt.

All patterns of play share common principles:

1. apply maximum concentration and group participation in play;
2. try to get possession of the ball, especially in the midfield and in defense;
3. shake off your marking player in order to be available for a pass from your teammate;
4. take few risks in the defensive phase;
5. take maximum care in marking the opponent, especially in the last 18 yards;
6. do not give away possession of the ball;
7. give the ball to your team-mate with a pass on his stride;
8. anticipate the tackle or interception when you are sure you will be successful, otherwise it is better to play for time;
9. if possible, avoid hurried low, sliding tackles, especially when the opponent has good skills;
10. apply pressure in the right way;
11. play with as much performance speed as possible; in particular, the defenders must be able to slow down, spread out, cut down the spaces, be aggressive.

Advantages:

1. defensive stability, guaranteed by 1 sweeper + 4 players;
2. compactness along the length of the field;
3. calmness in the defense, thanks to markings and coverings.

Disadvantages:

1. sometimes, inferiority in numbers on the sides of the field;
2. the midfield runs into difficulties when the opposing team plays with only one forward; in this case the defender with better skills must support the midfield;
3. central attacks outnumber attacks on the wings.

The importance of pressure

Like all "zone-play" patterns, the "5:3:2" also needs some typically defensive weapons like pressure.

If the side defenders are left on their own, they may run into difficulties: therefore they need the support of the right side and left side midfielders, followed by the support of their section's team-mates in a subsequent order, to regain the possession of the ball.

Also the forwards must apply pressure to the opposing defenders with the ball: in this way situations of inferiority in numbers can be avoided.

To apply pressure the following characteristics are required:
- high endurance;
- quickness of action;
- individual technical-tactical skills;
- good timing in the challenges;
- ability to spot the area of the field where pressure can best be applied.

Advantages and disadvantages of pressure

A. Advantages when you do not have possession of the ball:
1. opportunity to make up for teammates' mistakes;
2. greater involvement of the players in the match;
3. greater ease in reinforcing the zones of the field;
4. opportunity to set free the opposite side of the field;
5. superiority in numbers around the ball;
6. double-teaming, off-side (by cutting the distances between the sections);
7. better chances of pressure in the attack.

B. Advantages when you have possession of the ball:
1. compact team;
2. impression that you are doing something more than the opponents;
3. shorter distances between the players, with a better chance for simple passes;
4. uniform distribution of the players on the field;
5. ease in the possession of the ball;
6. more chances to start a counterattack;
7. greater self-assurance.

C. Disadvantages:

1. difficulty in marking a player from one zone of the field to the other;
2. too much space behind the defense line, a consequence of the shortening of the team;
3. possible lack of inventiveness and unpredictability once the team has gained possession of the ball;
4. a more compact team advances more slowly when it gets possession of the ball;
5. need for more joint responsibility and self-sacrifice.

Pressure on the midfield

This is a mostly counterattack-oriented tactic. Once the ball is lost, all the players move back and place themselves slightly behind or in front of the midfield line. By doing so, the team that does not have possession of the ball has superiority in numbers and applies some of the fundamental rules of pressure:

1. it occupies an area close to the ball with more players;
2. it faces the opponent with single players or pairs, so as to induce him to make a mistake;
3. meanwhile, it marks the opponents to prevent them from receiving passes.

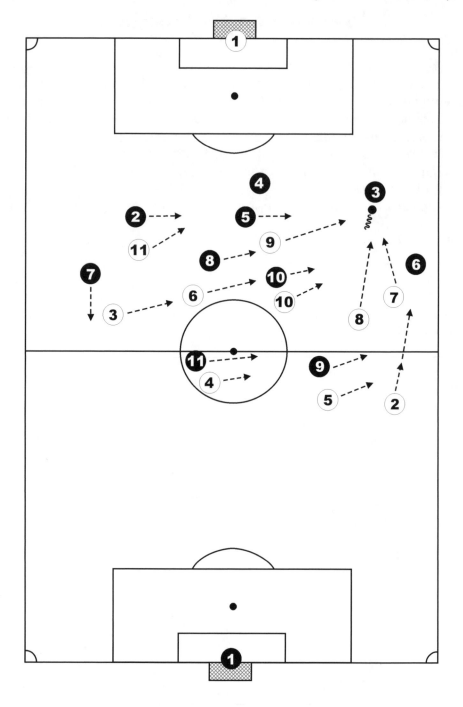

Diagram 42 - *Pressure on the midfield.*

Pressure in the attack

This is the most aggressive kind of pressure, but at the same time it is very dangerous too. Teams usually apply it when they are losing the match: the whole team moves forward, thus exposing itself to the opponents' counterattacks. Therefore, all the players must be determined in their movements applying simultaneous and resolute pressure.

The closest player to the opponent with the ball must attack him; the other players move towards the closest opponent to mark him tightly, while the most advanced forward attacks the sweeper to intercept possible back passes.

The following are the most frequent mistakes when applying pressure:
- the forwards attack the opponent, while the midfield and the defense do not participate;
- the defenders, midfielders and forwards do not move forward and do not retreat, so the distance between the players becomes too long;
- some players lack concentration and are tired, so they do not react as they should;
- too many fouls in the attacking zone that interrupt the effectiveness of pressure;
- the sweeper remains too far behind in his own half of the field;
- the defenders lack quickness.

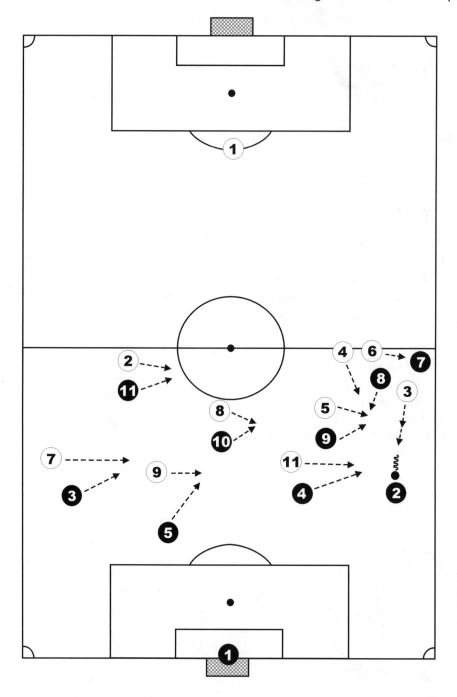

B - Pressure in the attack.

How to avoid pressure

Play over the midfield with long passes and follow the ball with the whole team.

Double-teaming in the "5:3:2"

This is a defensive tactical movement aimed at gaining possession of the ball or intercepting one of the opponents' passes. It can be carried out in any part of the field, provided that the sections of the team are at an equal distance. In basketball it is carried out on the sides but in soccer, on a larger field, it can be carried out also in the central area; of course, it has greater chances of success on the wings as the sideline acts as an extra defender.

Double-teaming requires clearness of mind and cleverness: if applied rashly it only produces continuous fouls, with ensuing disciplinary measures. Through coaching the tactical automatic movement and awareness of the double-teaming players can be improved: they must not attack the opponent simultaneously, but one after the other in order to avoid useless fouls (one of them attacks, the other plays for time).

As a general rule, double-teaming is applied to the opponent with the ball in those parts of the field where it can be more successful.

For example, a good area to apply it is on the wings: the player with the ball should not have any way out, caught in between the sideline and the two opponents. But also in this case there are some considerations to keep in mind: if the player with the ball has good skills, maximum care must be taken not to be both beaten one on one at the same time and leave the rest of the team in inferiority in numbers. The team-mates of the players who double-team must always shift to mark the opponents who have been left temporarily free. Double teaming can be carried out in the attack, midfield and defense zones.

Off-side

In the 5:3:2 off-side is usually applied only on particular occasions, due to the tactical characteristic of this pattern (two central defenders, a sweeper, two side players). In certain play situations, however, the players must be able to apply this defensive tactic.
Off-side is mostly applied in the following cases:

1. While the opposing forward penetrates in depth: with a sign, the sweeper starts the movement and the defenders sprint forward, while the midfielders apply pressure on the opponent with the ball; the goalkeeper, in turn, moves to the role of "sweeper" to intercept any opponents that may penetrate.
   This tactical movement is mostly carried out in case of inferiority in numbers or when the team needs to catch up;

2. Upon the clearance from the defense: on the occasion of crosses into the penalty area cleared by the defense (for example, on corner-kicks), the defender who has kicked the ball moves forward towards its direction, followed by all the team-mates of the defensive line and directly tackling the opponent with the ball.

3. When play is restarted: when there is a free-kick on the wing meant to send the ball into the penalty area for a forward's header, at the moment the ball is kicked the defending team sprints forward towards the opposing half of the field, thus cutting off and leaving the opponents off-side.

Off-side must be applied moderately, with good timing, cleverness and by surprise.

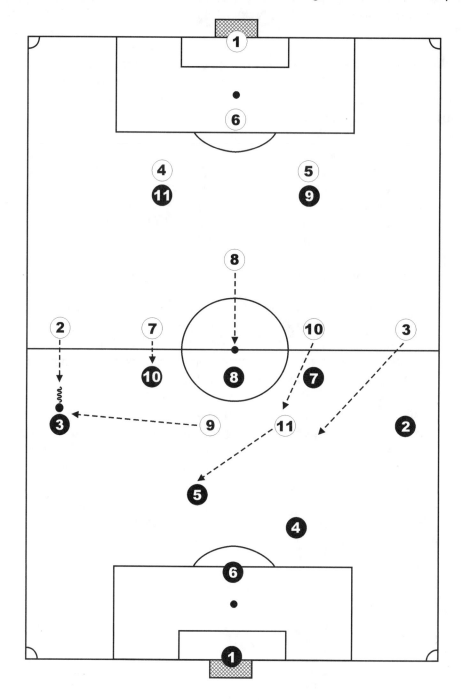

Diagram 44 - *SCHEME A: double-teaming in the attack zone.*

The opposing player 3 comes out of his penalty area with the ball and is faced by player 2 and 9, an example of double-teaming on the wing. Player 11 shifts to opposing player 5 to prevent a back pass from opposing player 3.

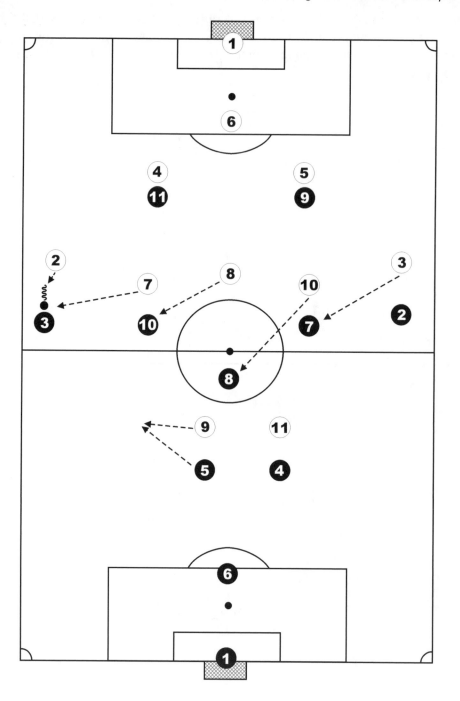

Diagram 45 - *SCHEME B: double-teaming in the midfield zone.*

Opposing player 3 is faced by player 2 and player 7, double-teaming on the wing. Player 8 shifts to opposing player 10, player 10 to opposing player 8 and player 3 to opposing player 7, while player 9 marks opposing player 5 to prevent a back pass from opposing player 3.

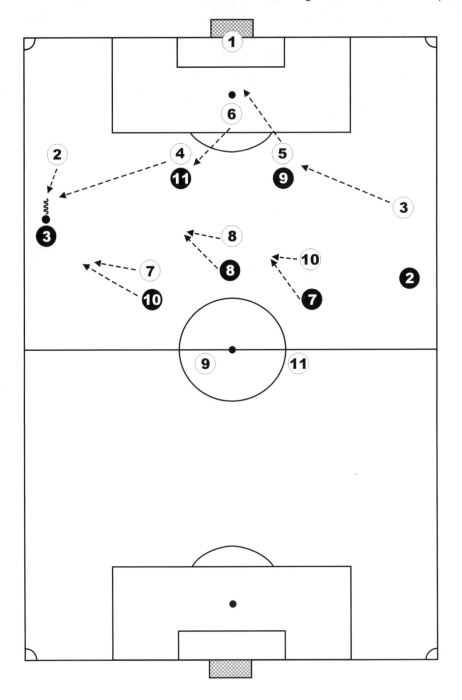

Diagram 46 - SCHEME C: double-teaming in the defense zone.

Opposing player 3 is faced by players 2 and 4, double-teaming on the wing; player 6 shifts to opposing player 11, player 5 to the position of sweeper, player 3 to opposing player 9. Player 7 follows opposing player 10 to prevent a back pass from opposing player 3.

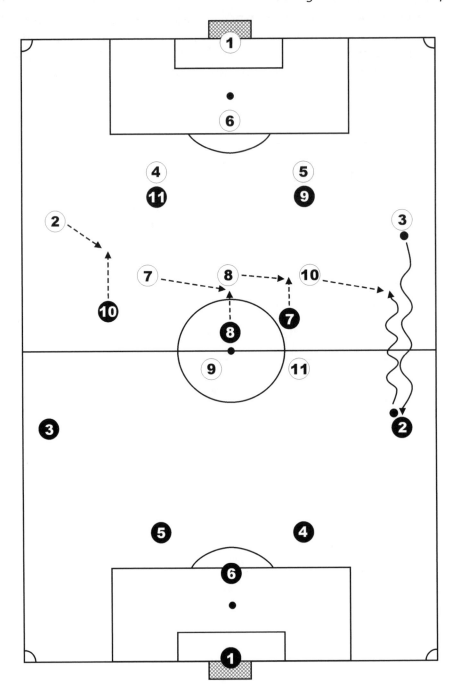

Diagram 47 - *Exercise for a "5-player" defense.*

Player 3 moves forward with the ball; he loses it after being tackled by opposing player 2, who counter-attacks. Player 10 shifts to him; the same movement is carried out by player 8 who shifts to mark opposing player 7; player 7 shifts to opposing player 8 and player 2 to opposing mid-fielder 10.

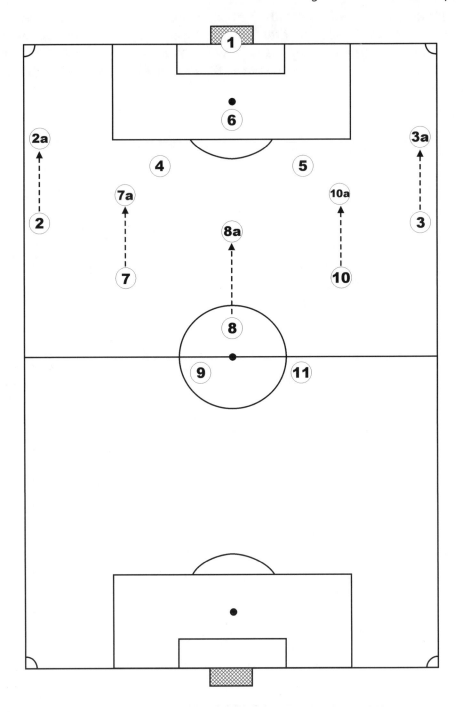

***Diagram 48** - The "5:3:2" (in the defensive phase).*

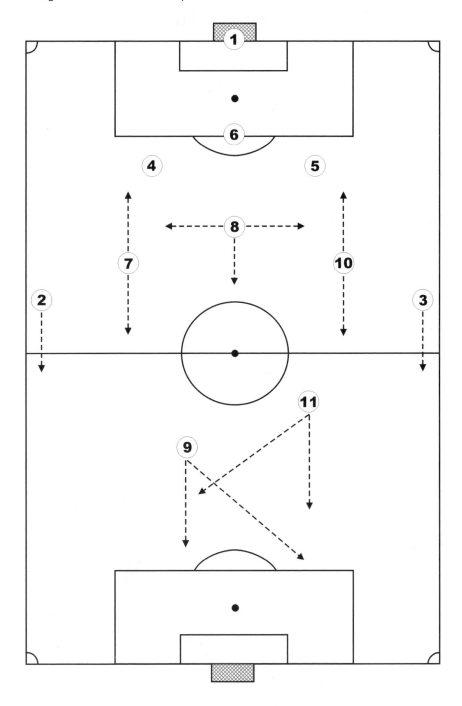

Diagram 49 - The "3:5:2" (when the team has possession of the ball).

The "5:3:2" against other patterns

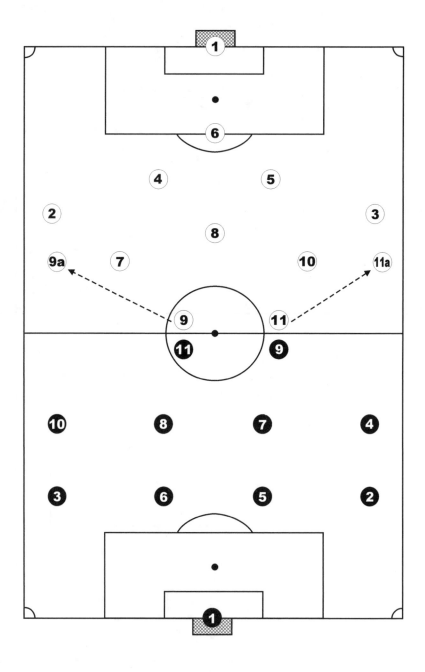

Diagram 50 - The "5:3:2" versus the "4:4:2".

The "4:4:2" has one more player in the midfield: he can get the "5:3:2" into trouble when he has possession of the ball. This problem can be solved by pulling back to the side player 9 or 11 in turns, thus restoring the equality in numbers in the midfield.

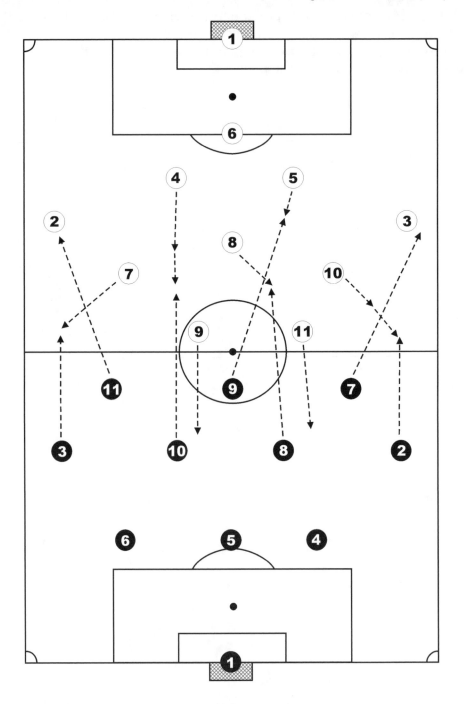

Diagram 51 - *The "5:3:2" versus the "3:4:3".*

Player 2 and 3 plus a central defender, either player 4 or 5 (usually the least skilled), mark the three forwards.

The other central defender moves to the midfield.

Player 7 and player 10 play on the sides: they take the action forward and control opposing players 3 and 2 when they advance.

Players 4 and 8 control the center of the field and forwards 9 and 11 try to get the opposing defensive zone into trouble with their movements.

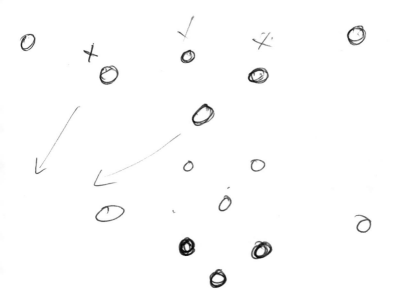

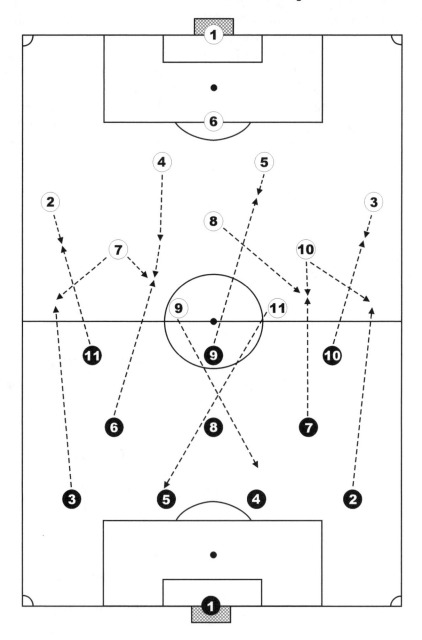

Diagram 52 - The "5:3:2" versus the "4:3:3".
   What we have just said about the "3:4:3" applies to this scheme also.

EXERCISES

Coaching examples

EXERCISE 1

❏ Key points

- coaching reaction abilities and sprinting speed;
- search for position and attack on the opponent with the ball

❏ Organization

- Two 6-player groups carry out two different exercises in turn. The two groups exchange tasks and positions after about 15-20 minutes.
- Each 6-player group is divided into two teams of three players each.
- Group A plays in a specific zone of the field, near the midfield line (zone of pressure on the midfield).
- Group B plays in a 40x30-yard space, with the goalkeeper defending the goal.

❏ Group A

- *Pressure on a pass*
  One of the two 3-player groups (group in white) jogs along one half of the field with the ball.
  The players of the other group (in black) run slowly in the other half, individually. The player with the ball suddenly passes it to an opponent on the other side of the field, pretending to make a wrong pass or clearance.
  This pass is the signal for all the team-mates in white to go near the closest player in black and mark him. The player in black with the ball must try to dribble and keep the ball as long as possible, resist

ing the group in white that is trying to gain the possession of the ball by pressure.

When white gains possession, both groups go back to their starting positions. Now it is the group in black to start the game, and after a short phase of relaxation a new pressure action begins.

- *Key points of coaching:*
  a. sprint and reaction ability;
  b. tackle with the opposing dribbler;
  c. group understanding.

❏ Group B

- *Pressure on pass with shot at goal*
  Same development as with group A.
  The players in white move together in the penalty area, acting as a team under pressure.
  The attacking group, in black, waits in the other half of the field.
  The action starts when the goalkeeper passes the ball to a player in white.
  Before winning the ball, the attacking team in black must adequately and closely apply pressure on the opponents, especially on the one with the ball.
  The team in white must break free from this pressure situation and dribble the ball beyond the goal line. Once they have won the ball the players in black shoot at goal.
  At the end of the action the groups go back to the starting position. After ten actions the teams exchange tasks and positions.

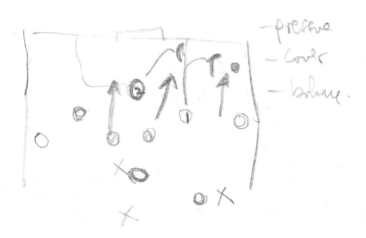

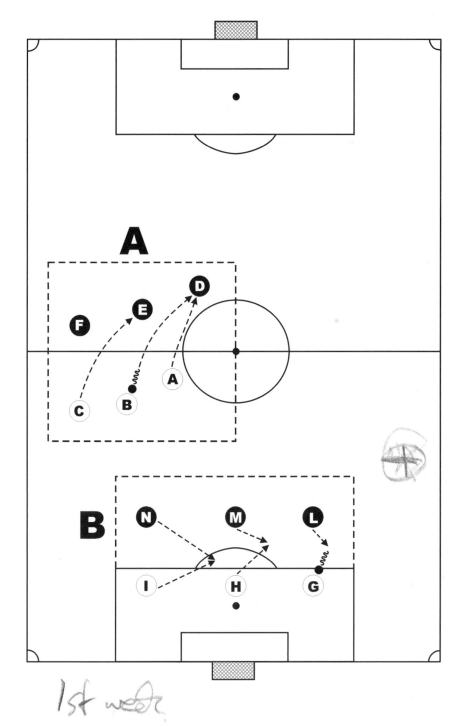

1st week

Diagram 53 - *Exercise 1.*

EXERCISE 2

❏ Key points of coaching

- quick movement towards the ball;
- marking the closest opponent correctly;
- taking care of unmarked opponents;
- forward movement of the sweeper;
- aggressiveness in tackles.

❏ Organization

- On the midfield line, a 35-yard long zone is marked by cones.
- Two 5-player teams play on two-thirds of the field, with goalkeepers defending their goal.
- Team B has an extra player with the role of sweeper.

❏ Development

- Play is always started by team A, which has the ball and is inferior in numbers.
  The players of team B must apply pressure on the opponents, if possible by double-teaming the opponent with the ball, preventing team A from advancing towards their goal and winning the ball as soon as possible. Once team B has the possession of the ball it must quickly shoot at goal (counterattack).

❏ Advice

- If the actions are too long and the players do not seem determined in their play, then the coach should interrupt the action and team A should restart play.

❏ Variations

- Team B plays on two smaller goals.
- Play zones are moved according to certain key points of the opposing pressure.

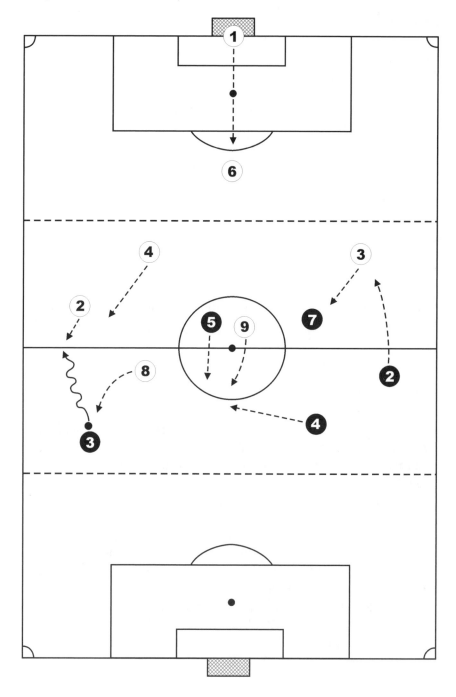

Diagram 54 - Exercise 2.

EXERCISE 3

❏ Key points of coaching

  • preparing the players to intensify play in the tactical sector (warm-up)
  • increasing resistance to play;
  • quick understanding of the play situation and of the opponents' actions;
  • alternation of pace between a waiting stance and a determined attack;

❏ Organization

  • On the midfield line, a 35-yard long zone is marked by cones.
  • Two teams with an equal number of players are lined up on the field and the ball is given to team A.

❏ Development

  • The two teams start to move together in the midfield, while the players of team A pass the ball to one another.
    In this phase team A is not pressured. Meanwhile, the players of team B start to move so as to always have an opponent in close proximity and, when they have the right opportunity, they take turns on the opponents.
    As soon as a player of team B resolutely pressures the opponent with the ball, thus obliging him to a direct challenge, for all his teammates this is the signal to start pressure. Each player of team B must immediately face his own opponent. Team A must resist the opponents' pressure as long as possible and keep possession of the ball. Once team B wins the ball, the action is interrupted for a short relaxing phase; then, team B restarts the game with a sequence of simple passes.

❏ Variations

  • Once the ball has been won, it must be passed to the goalkeeper.
  • Once the ball has been won, it must be quickly dribbled beyond the end line of the zone.

EXERCISE 4: "4 on 4" - "2 on 2" - "3 on 2"

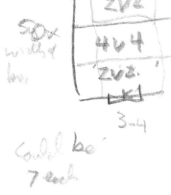

❏ Key points of coaching

- quick understanding of the play situations;
- behavior determined by the zones of play;
- quick retreat and change of positions;
- goals scored with superiority in numbers.

❏ Organization

- Two 8-player teams are lined up each with a goalkeeper defending its goal, on a 70-yard long field as wide as the penalty area.
- The field is divided into three zones marked by cones: 1, 2 and 3 are respectively the attack, central and defense zones. The central zone and the zone in front of the goal are a little longer.
- The two 8-player teams are arranged as follows in the different zones:
  a. in the central zone the players play four versus four;
  b. in the two zones in front of the goals the players play two versus two.

❏ Development

- The play starts in the central zones where there are 4 players playing against 4 opponents. At the coach's signal, the team with the ball gives it to one of its players in the attack zone, to start a quick attack to the goal. On this pass, a teammate from the central zone can immediately sprint to the attack zone, so as to create a "3 on 2" attack situation in front of the goal and score a goal.
  After the shot at goal, one of the three attackers must immediately go back to the central zone to restore the "4 on 4" situation and mark the opponents.
  When the defenders win the ball in the defense zone, the three opposing forwards must immediately attack them in a "3 on 2" situation so as to win back possession of the ball and shoot at goal. The defenders try to free themselves from the marking player and pass the ball to one of their teammates in the midfield, who can start a counterattack thanks to the superiority in numbers.
  Three 7-minute periods are played, alternating with a 5-minute

active relaxation phase. At the end of each period the players of each team exchange zones.

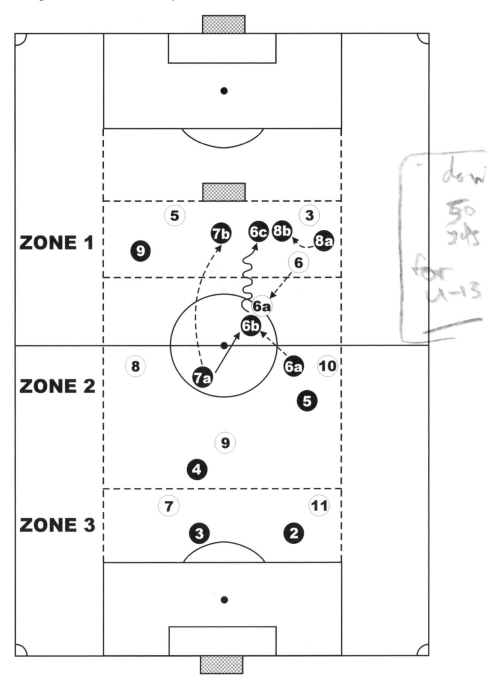

Diagram 55 - Exercise 4.

EXERCISE 5

❏ Key points of coaching

  • improvement of the pressure tactics;
  • passing by degrees from pressure on the midfield to pressure in
    the attack;
  • improvement of shots at goal.

❏ Organization

  • Two teams with an equal number of players are lined up on two-
    thirds of the field. The field, marked by cones, is divided into a
    central zone and two attack zones in front of the goals.
  • The boundary lines between the central zone and the attack zones
    make up the off-side lines too.

❏ Development

  • The two teams apply determined pressure on the opponent. The
    penalty area cannot be crossed and goals can be scored only
    according to the following rules:
  a. Side play (deep pass, back pass), deep and level passes towards
      the goal zone or back passes towards the penalty spot. The
      goals must be scored by directly taking advantage of the pass-
      es, with low-ground shots.
  b. Shots from a distance from outside the penalty area.
  c. All the players of the opposing team must advance up to the
      central zone between the two off-side lines.

Two 15-minute periods are played, alternating with a 5-minute active
relaxation phase. In the meantime the coach can give some directions
for possible corrections.

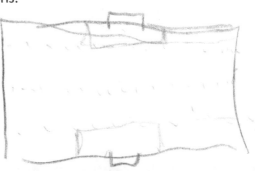

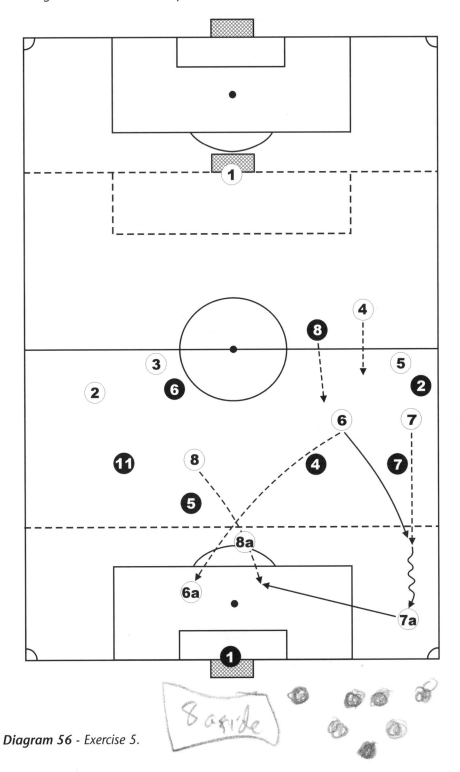

Diagram 56 - *Exercise 5.*

CHAPTER V

DEFENSIVE SCHEMES

EXERCISE WITH 3 DEFENDERS VERSUS 2 FORWARDS
(superiority in numbers)

One half of the field is divided into two equal parts (two quarters of the whole field).

Two defenders versus two forwards are placed in one quarter; the third defender is in the other quarter and intervenes when needed, shifting the marking.

Defender 4 takes care of opponent 11, defender 2 faces opponent 9, defender 3 shifts to the position of sweeper in defensive covering.

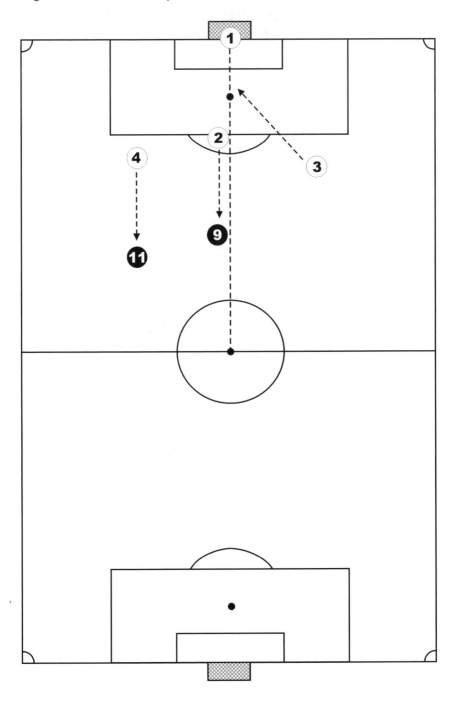

Diagram 57 - *Exercise with 3 defenders versus 2 forwards.*

EXERCISE WITH 4 DEFENDERS
VERSUS 3 FORWARDS
(superiority in numbers)

One half of the field is divided into two equal parts (two quarters of the whole field).

Three defenders versus two forwards are placed in one quarter; the fourth defender is in the other quarter and intervenes when needed, shifting the marking.

Opposing forward 11 dribbles past defender 2 and advances towards the penalty area; defender 3 leaves his direct opponent 9 in order to stop the advance of opponent 11; defender 4, playing as a sweeper up to now, immediately shifts to mark opponent 9, and his position is taken up by the fourth defender, player 5, with a diagonal movement; opposing forward 9 is thus left free from marking, but in this particular situation he does not represent an impending danger to the defense.

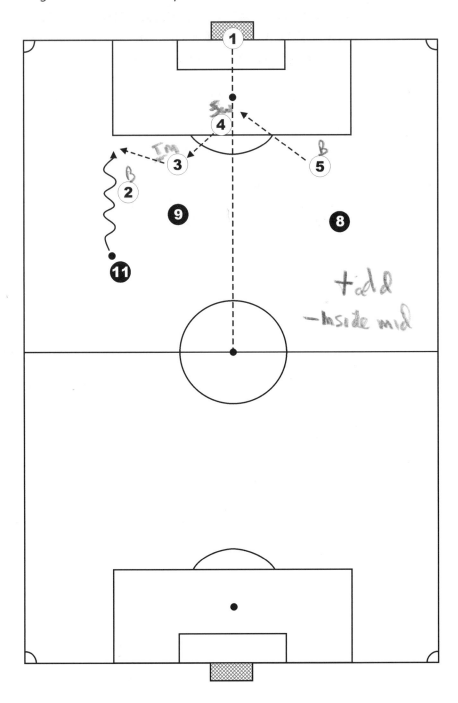

Diagram 58 - *Exercise with 4 defenders versus 3 forwards.*

DEFENSIVE EXERCISE AGAINST THE OPPONENTS' ATTACK COMING FROM THE RIGHT SIDE OF THE FIELD
(shifting the marking and defensive diagonal movements)

Opponent 7 dribbles past defender 3 and advances towards the penalty area; defender 5 shifts to mark him, while his position is taken up by "sweeper" 6. Defender 4 shifts to the position of "sweeper" by a diagonal defensive movement, while side defender 2 takes up defender 4's former position by the same movement.

Of course these defensive movements leave opposing forward 3 free from marking on the left side, but in such a situation he is far from play and does not represent an impending danger to the defense.

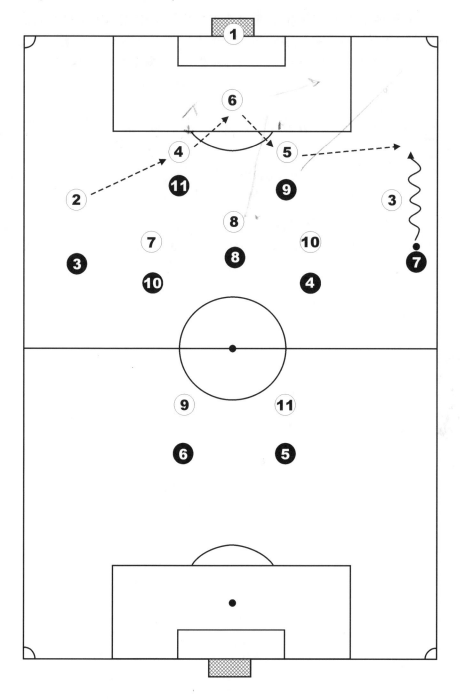

Diagram 59 - *Defensive exercise against the opponents' attack coming from the right side of the field.*

DEFENSIVE EXERCISE AGAINST THE OPPONENTS' ATTACK COMING FROM THE LEFT SIDE OF THE FIELD
(shifting the marking and defensive diagonal movements)

Opponent 3 dribbles past defender 2 and advances towards the penalty area; defender 4 shifts to mark him, while his position is taken up by "sweeper" 6.

Defender 5 shifts to the position of "sweeper" by a diagonal defensive movement, while defender 3 takes up defender 5's former position by the same movement.

Of course these defensive movements leave opposing forward 7 free from marking on the right side, but in such a situation he is far from play and does not represent an impending danger to the defense.

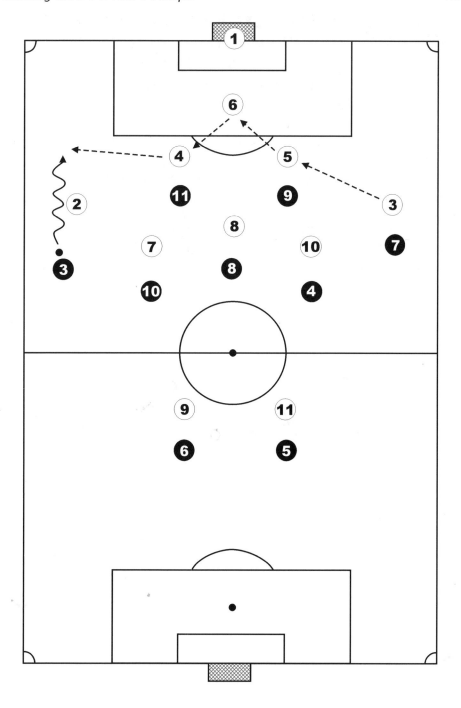

Diagram 60 - *Defensive exercise against the opponents' attack coming from the left side of the field.*

DEFENSIVE EXERCISE AGAINST
THE OPPONENTS' ATTACK
COMING FROM THE CENTER
(shifting the marking, defensive diagonal
movements, pressure and off-side)

Opposing midfielder 8 dribbles past midfielder 8 and advances towards the penalty area; "sweeper" 6 moves forward to face him, helped by defenders 4 and 5 who both converge on opponent 8, thus leaving their direct opponents 9 and 11. Side defenders 2 and 3 shift the marking on opponents 9 and 11, or the latter are left off-side if opponent 8 makes a deep pass. In this case, opposing side forwards 7 and 3 are left free from marking, but in such a situation their position on the field does not represent an impending danger to the defense.

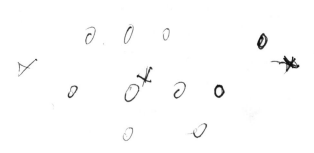

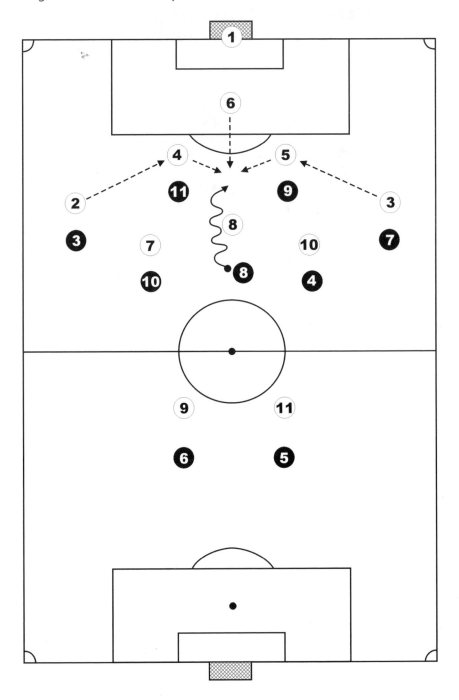

Diagram 61 - *Defensive exercise against the opponents' attack coming from the center.*

DEFENSIVE EXERCISE AGAINST TEAMS
WITH ONLY ONE FORWARD

It is useless to play with three fixed defenders against teams with only one forward: at least one of the three defenders, the one with better skills, should play in the midfield and be helped by the whole team.

Defender 6 takes care of opposing forward 9 and, if needed, he is helped by defender 4. Defender 2 either takes care of opponent 11 (option "a") or shifts to defender 4's former position (option "b") to face the advance of opposing midfielder 10.

Defender 5 moves to the midfield and plays in the zone of opponent 8; defender 3 makes the same movement and plays in the zone of opponent 7 (option "a").

Defenders 2 and 3 must always be ready to carry out diagonal defensive movements (option "b") to stop the opposing midfielders' possible advance.

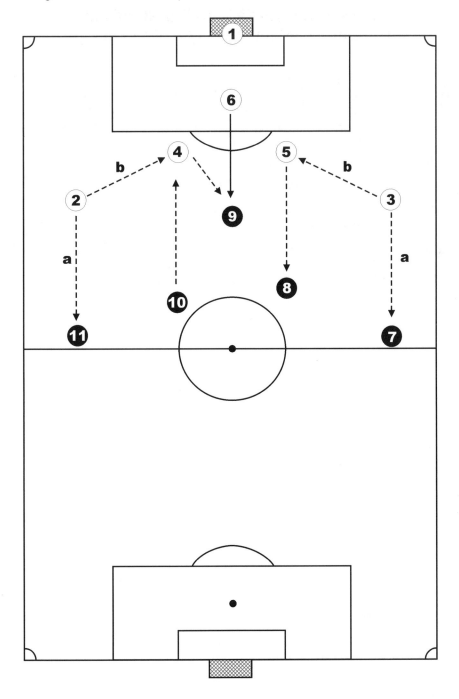

Diagram 62 - *Defensive exercise against teams with only one forward.*

5 ON 7 DEFENSIVE EXERCISE
(Inferiority in numbers, double-teaming)

Opponent 8 advances with the ball and makes a pass to his team-mate 3 (who is penetrating into the left side) when "sweeper" 6 faces him.

Defender 4 shifts to mark opponent 3, thus obliging his team-mates to shift the marking on the opponents who are in the most dangerous position at that moment: defender 6 shifts to opponent 11, defender 5 to opponent 8 and defender 3 to opponent 9, leaving the zone where they belong as this does not represent an impending danger in such a situation.

This exercise can be varied by increasing the number of players in both teams, while at the same time respecting the principle of the inferiority in numbers: for example, 6 on 8, 7 on 9, 8 on 10. In this way the players get used to facing any situation of inferiority in numbers.

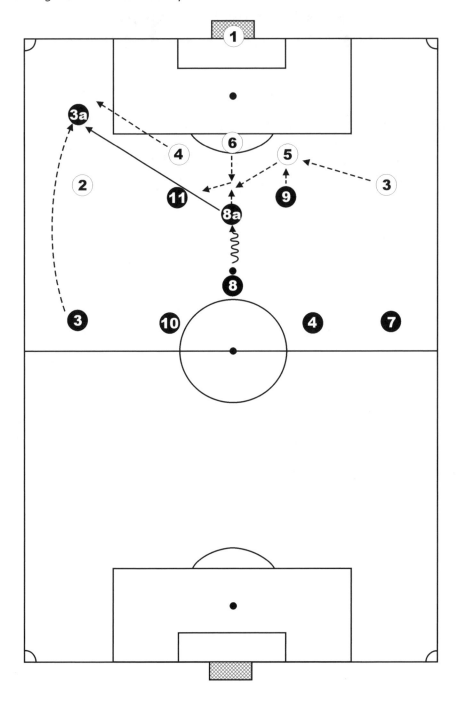

Diagram 63 - 5 on 7 defensive exercise.

DEFENSIVE CLEARANCE ON
PRESSURE FROM THE OPPONENTS

Defender 2 has the ball; opponent 3 applies pressure on him, and so do opponents 11, 8 and 9 on defenders 4, 6 and 5 respectively. Defender 2 has two options: either he makes a long pass along the side to his team-mate 9 (option "a") or he makes a back pass to his goalkeeper, who must immediately pass it on to his team-mate 3 on the other side (option "b").

If this clearance is carried out quickly it might produce a dangerous counterattack.

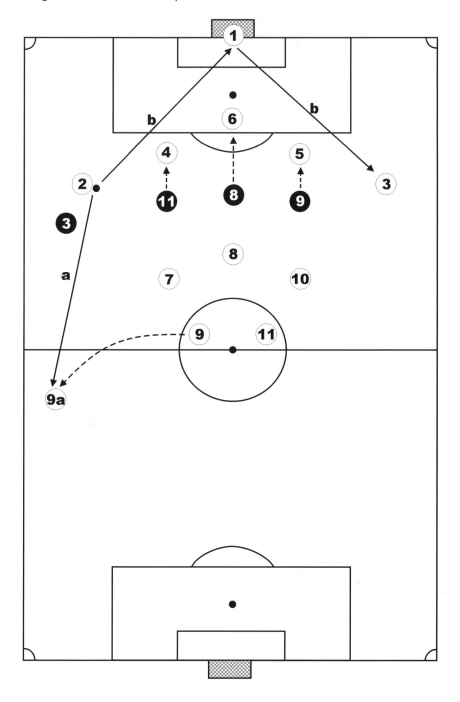

Diagram 64 - *Defensive clearance on pressure from the opponents.*

OVERLAPPING ON THE LEFT
IN THE DEFENSIVE PHASE

Sweeper 6 has the ball and passes it to player 5, who passes it on to player 3 and overlaps on the wing.

Player 3 passes the ball to midfielder 10, who makes a pass to player 5, now in position 5a.

Player 5 advances, then crosses to forwards 9 and 11 who, in order to puzzle the opposing defenders, criss-cross while running towards the penalty area.

4-2-4.

Ridley   Manson

Gruneau

Simmons   Kfangle

Furnen   Clarke

Gillied   (minima)   Keefer/miller

Colle

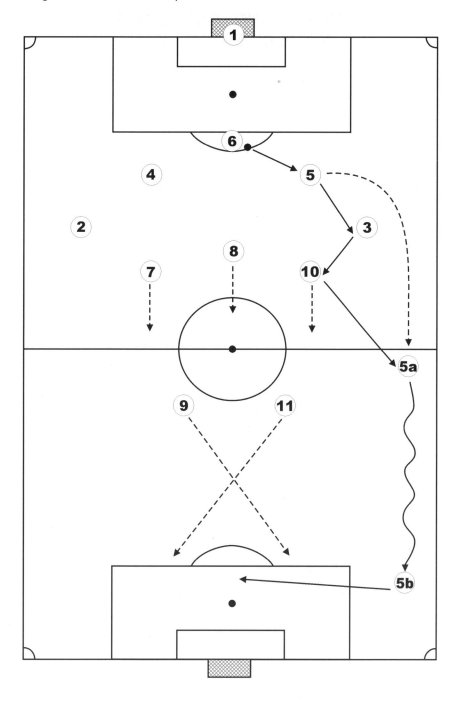

Diagram 65 - *Overlapping on the left in the defensive phase.*

OVERLAPPING ON THE RIGHT
IN THE DEFENSIVE PHASE

Sweeper 6 has the ball and passes it to player 4, who after passing it on to player 2 overlaps on the wing.

Player 2 passes the ball to midfielder 7, who makes a pass to player 4, now in position 5a.

Player 5 advances, then crosses to forwards 9 and 11 who, in order to puzzle the opposing defenders, criss-cross while running towards the penalty area.

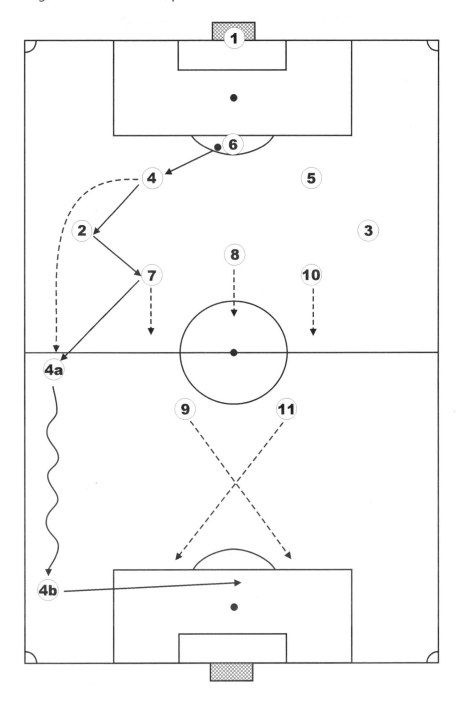

Diagram 66 - Overlapping on the right in the defensive phase.

OVERLAPPING WITH DOUBLE OPTION IN THE DEFENSIVE PHASE

Player 6 has the ball and passes it to player 5; player 5 passes it on to player 3 and overlaps on the left wing.

Player 3 makes a pass to player 8, who then has two options: either be passes the ball to player 5, now in position 5a (option "a") or he passes it to player 2, who has advanced to position 2a. After receiving the ball, player 2 advances towards the goal line and crosses to his team-mates 9 and 11 who, after criss-crossing while running, are now in position 9a and 11a (option "b"). This option is shown in the following diagram.

Fwds	Omids	Imids(O)	Imids(D)	Backs
Manson	Gruneau	Simmons	Clarke	Cotter
Krangle	Close-H.	Ridley	miller	Keefer
Bjurman	Forward	Forman	~~Bjurman~~	Gillard
Ridley	Ridley	Darwin	Ridley	miller
Symons	Chambers		Darwin	Bjurman
Forward	Darwin		Bjurman	Ridley
Chambers	Cotter/Gillard			
Gruneau	Bjurman			
Cotter				

- Chambers

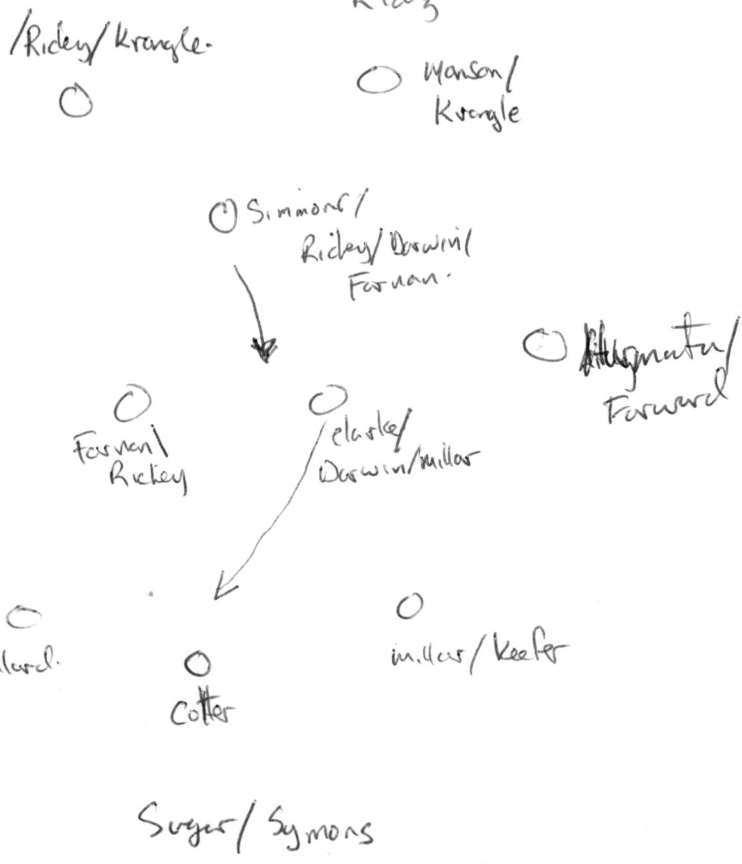

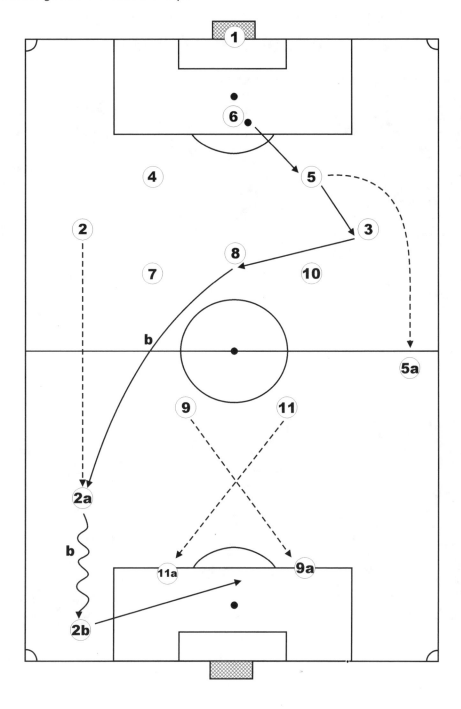

Diagram 67 - *Overlapping with double option in the defensive phase.*

Coaching Books from REEDSWAIN

#785:
**Complete Book of
Soccer Restart Plays**
*by Mario Bonfanti and
Angelo Pereni*
$14.95

#154:
Coaching Soccer
by Bert van Lingen
$14.95

#177:
PRINCIPLES OF
Brazilian Soccer
by José Thadeu Goncalves
in cooperation with Prof. Julio Mazzei
$16.95

#185:
**Conditioning
for Soccer**
Dr. Raymond Verheijen
$19.95

#244:
Coaching the 4-4-2
by Marziali and Mora
$14.95

#765:
**Attacking Schemes
and Training
Exercises**
*by Eugenio Fascetti and
Romedio Scaia*
$14.95

Call REEDSWAIN 1-800-331-5191

Coaching Books from REEDSWAIN

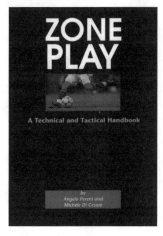

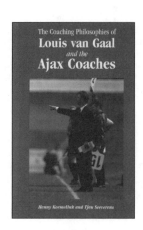
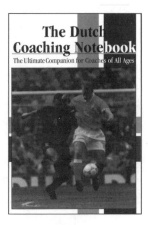

Coaching Books from REEDSWAIN

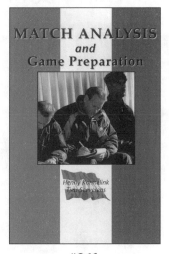
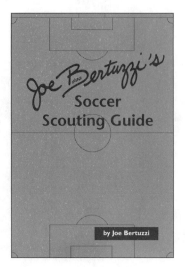
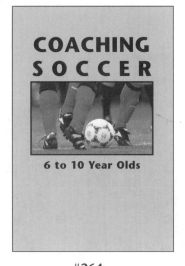